Praise for *Deeper*

One word comes to mind when I think of D[...]
one word I'd use to describe this book? *Timeless.* [...] Denise doesn't
color outside the lines in order to be cool. She loves God's Word, knows God's
Word, and articulates God's ways in a timeless, beautiful fashion. If you long to
know God on a deep and profound level, Denise would tell you to spend time
in His Word. Absolutely true. But I'd also say, take your time working through
the pages of this book. Denise serves as a wise, godly mentor. She tackles tough
questions and offers fresh insight, all at the same time. This book is a gift to
God's people.

> —**Susie Larson,** national speaker, talk radio host,
> and author of *Your Powerful Prayers*

Do you want to open the Bible but don't know where to begin? Or does the size
and depth of God's Word intimidate you? If these questions have crossed your
mind, *Deeper Waters* is for you. Denise's fresh look at God's Word removes that
intimidation factor. She gently leads you into the Bible and takes you on a per-
spective-changing, life-transforming journey through its pages. Her personal
stories and creative teaching style, combined with her biblical depth, transform the Bible from a textbook to a workbook. Denise equips you with practical tools to read your Bible confidently; know God intimately; apply what you
learn personally; and most importantly, take what you have learned into your
corner of the world.

> —**Wendy Blight,** Proverbs 31 First 5 Writing Team, speaker, Bible teacher,
> and author of *I Know His Name, Living So That*, and
> *Hidden Joy in a Dark Corner*

From the opening pages of this beautiful book, you cannot miss Denise
Hughes's passion for God's Word. Prepare your heart, because that passion is
contagious. Dive into *Deeper Waters* and drench yourself in the saving grace, tremendous power, and redeeming love of God. This book is a treasure.

> —**Jennifer Dukes Lee,** author of *The Happiness Dare* and *Love Idol*

In a world searching for purpose and meaning, Denise Hughes is a teacher of
truth and a storyteller of beautiful redemption. She distills the details of Scripture with a voice that rings clear, revelatory, and applicable. *Deeper Waters* is a
journey you don't want to miss.

> —**Shelly Miller,** author of *Rhythms of Rest*

Read this book with a Bible and box of tissues nearby. Part memoir and part Bible study, Denise's book will touch your heart. Her beautifully chosen words will bring you closer to the God of all comfort.

—**Arlene Pellicane,** author of *31 Days to Becoming a Happy Mom*

The absolute best way to hear God's voice is through His Word, both the words we read in the Bible and by taking the time—like the scribes of old—to write the Word ourselves. In ancient times, the scribes knew the Word intimately because they both studied it and wrote it out. Reading Denise J. Hughes's marvelous new book, *Deeper Waters*, makes me feel as if I'm sitting at the feet of a scribe whose gentle manner and profound wisdom stirs a fresh hunger in me to study God's Word. Denise employs a nonthreatening, easy-to-understand method of study. Her gentle encouragement and practical wisdom are framed by deeply moving and transparent stories of her own life, hurts, doubts, and seasons of brokenness every woman can relate to. Nothing will transform your life more than hearing the voice of God. Let Denise take you by the hand and guide you on your journey and get ready to have your life transformed.

—**Kate Battistelli,** author of *Growing Great Kids* and mother of GRAMMY award-winning artist Francesca Battistelli.

I can't think of people I know whose lives seem to be characterized by deeper waters without thinking of Denise Hughes. A woman who has walked through difficulty as well as triumph, she has done the hard work of digging deep to find the truth of God in all of it. She is soft-spoken but strong, gentle, and wise, and I trust her heart and her ability not only to invite you into the life-changing truth of God's Word, but to help uncover it as well. A gem of a writer, teacher, and friend, I cannot say enough good things about Denise and the works of her hands.

—**Logan Wolfram,** author of *Curious Faith* and CEO of the Allume Conference

As a Bible teacher and pastor's wife, I am thankful for writers like Denise who faithfully and consistently point us to the truth of Scripture. As a friend, I'm thankful for women like Denise who honestly and graciously point me to Jesus. *Deeper Waters* is a gift to all of us who long for more of Christ and His Word. Denise has opened the Word and invited us to join her on the journey to abide fully and deeply in Christ. And we can be sure we have a thoughtful guide who has known the faithfulness and generosity of the One about whom she writes.

—**Teri Lynne Underwood,** author of *Praying for Girls*

Deeper Waters

DENISE J. HUGHES

HARVEST HOUSE PUBLISHERS
EUGENE, OREGON

Cover by Darren Welch Design

Cover Image © Natali Snailcat / Shutterstock

Denise J. Hughes is published in association with the literary agency of The Steve Laube Agency, LLC, 24 W. Cambelback Rd. A-635, Phoenix, Arizona 85013.

Names and details have been changed to protect the privacy of certain individuals.

DEEPER WATERS

Contents

The Voice We Hear 9

Part One ~ Determining in Your Heart
Ezra had *determined* in his heart...Ezra 7:10

1. The Exile We Know 19

2. The Lament We Feel 29

3. The Decision We Make 35

4. The Challenges We Face 43

Part Two ~ To Study God's Word
...to *study* the law of the Lord...Ezra 7:10

5. The Water We Need 53

6. The Way We Wait 63

7. The Time We Spend 73

8. The Words We Write 85

9. The Prayers We Keep 93

Part Three ~ To Obey God's Voice
...to *obey* it...Ezra 7:10

10. The Truth We Live 107

11. The Compass We Follow 117

12. The Failure We Grieve 125

13. The Purpose We Reclaim 137

14. The Grace We Give. 151

Part Four ~ To Teach God's Precepts

...and *teach* its statutes and ordinances in Israel...Ezra 7:10

15. The Women We Welcome 163

16. The Roots We Plant 173

17. The Story We Share 181

18. The Song We Sing 193

Epilogue ~ Starting Today

Read It: 365-Day Bible Reading Plan 203

Write It: Psalm 119. 215

Pray It: Prayers in the Bible. 239

Notes 243

Acknowledgments 247

About the Author. 249

To
Kendall
Your courage goes beyond all bounds.

As the crowd was pressing in on Jesus to hear God's word,
He was standing by Lake Gennesaret.
He saw two boats at the edge of the lake;
the fishermen had left them and were washing their nets.
He got into one of the boats, which belonged to Simon,
and asked him to put out a little from the land.
Then He sat down and was teaching the crowds from the boat.
When He had finished speaking, He said to Simon,
"Put out into deep water and let down your nets for a catch."…
When they did this, they caught a great number of fish…
Then they brought the boats to land, left everything,
and followed Him.

LUKE 5:1-11

The Voice We Hear

Wise words are like deep waters.

Proverbs 18:4 NLT

My kids looked forward to every Tuesday for no other reason than I had promised on those nights not to cook. On Tuesdays their father drove straight from work to a nearby university to pursue his graduate studies in Christian apologetics. So while my husband investigated the deep things of God, I put a frozen pizza in the oven and watched *American Idol* on TV with our children.

I admit I found the televised singing contest partly amusing. Some of the auditions were indeed humorous, if not absurd. But I also found it unsettling how so many Americans delighted in laughing at people who couldn't sing well. All of the sudden we were no longer spectators; we were judges—chomping on pepperoni while pointing at a screen. "She goes flat on the low notes." "He can belt it, but he does that weird thing with his bangs." On and on we'd go.

Still, the popular show was giving its audience something worth coming back for, something more than a few laughs and a remote chance at stardom. The singing contest was actually offering, in part, two essential elements in life: beauty and truth. We loved it when a contestant could really sing. The excitement of discovering a new, beautiful voice compelled us. And whenever the third judge spoke, we secretly appreciated his candor, even though his frankness often-times bordered rudeness. The winner gave us a voice of beauty; the third judge gave us a voice of truth, albeit a jaded form of it.

Why else would so many millions tune in? We are drawn by a voice of beauty. We are held by a voice of truth.

> We are drawn by a voice of beauty. We are held by a voice of truth.

Not just in music, but in literature too. Whenever I attend a large event for women, I observe dozens, and sometimes hundreds, of women waiting in line to have a few brief moments with their favorite author. There's nothing wrong with this, of course. It's natural to want to connect with the person whose voice spoke to them in some way. It reveals a basic human tendency we all share: Something inside us gravitates toward voices of beauty and truth.

We're influenced not only by the voices of popular singers and writers, but also by the voices of parents, teachers, coaches, pastors, neighbors, and even total strangers. For good or bad, voices influence us. And with the advent of the Internet, millions of voices contend for an audience every day. They vie for our attention. A few will be heard above the noise—mostly the ones that resemble, at least to some degree, an element of beauty and truth.

There's only one problem. Not every beautiful voice bears reliable truth. Some voices are a distant echo of truth, an alloyed measure of the real thing. So we must discern what is true from what is untrue, what is real from what is unreal. But how? What standard can we use to determine reliable truth?

When I was in high school, I attended my church's youth group. One night the youth pastor asked for a volunteer to come to the middle of the room. He held up a giant Snickers bar and told the volunteer he could have it if he could find it. But there were two caveats: (1) The volunteer would be blindfolded, and (2) everyone else in the room could only offer directions—such as turn around, go left, go right, reach up, bend down. The youth pastor blindfolded the volunteer and hid the candy bar where everyone else in the room could see. When he yelled "Go!" everyone began shouting. "Go left!" "Keep going!" "Reach up!" "Turn around!" But the blindfolded guy just stood in the middle of the room, paralyzed. With so much chaotic noise around him, he couldn't discern which voice to listen to.

The youth pastor quieted everyone down and asked the volunteer to choose one friend in the room to give him directions. With only one voice giving him directions, he found the candy bar within seconds. The youth pastor's point was clear. Many voices will compete for our attention, but we'll find our way when we choose to listen to the voice of a trusted Friend.

I have a dear friend whose son was born deaf. He couldn't hear his mama read storybooks to him. He couldn't hear her sing over him as he slept. He couldn't hear her warn him when he approached something dangerous. Shortly after his first birthday, he had surgery to receive cochlear implants. A few weeks after the surgery my friend and her husband drove their son to the audiologist. It was Activation Day, the day they would turn on their son's new ears.

> We find our path in life once we're listening to the voice that matters most.

In the video of those first few moments, you can see his little face look up in wonder the first time he hears the machine beeping. When the audiologist claps her hands, he touches the devices next to his ears. He's making the connection. Then his father leans in and speaks to him. For the first time he hears his father's voice. The boy turns his head and looks at his father, a smile lighting his sweet face.

Most of us can't recall the first moment we heard our parents' voices. We were only babies. But I can distinctly recall the first time I heard my Father's voice. It wasn't an audible voice, but it was as real as the air I breathed.

God's Word lay open before me. As I read the Bible, the words seemed to come alive on the page. It was July 31, 1990. My Activation Day.[1] From that day forward I chose my Father's voice to be my trusted guide—my soul's compass.

Throughout history men and women have experienced their own spiritual Activation Day—the day they first heard God speak to them.Sometimes God speaks to us through our circumstances. Sometimes He speaks to us through other people. Most of the time, however, God speaks to us through His Word. This book is about learning to hear God's voice through His Word so we can discern what is true from what is untrue. Because once we've heard the voice of our Father—the voice of the One who designed us and created a distinct purpose for us—we become like the blindfolded volunteer in my youth group who chose a friend to guide him. We find our path in life once we're listening to the voice that matters most.

In ancient times, before Jesus walked this earth, God spoke to His people primarily through prophets and priests. In every generation God raised up voices to communicate timeless truths. These voices called people back to truth, back to reality (and by "reality," I don't mean anything we observe on reality TV). The book you're holding now follows the life of one such priest.

Ezra was an out-of-work priest because he lived in Babylon as an exile. Since the temple back in Jerusalem had been destroyed, the job of a temple priest had become obsolete. The people in exile had to assimilate into their new culture and settle into a life far from their homeland. Coming from a priestly family, Ezra was well-educated and highly literate, so he procured a job somewhere in Babylonian government, serving as either a record keeper or some other official position that required the rare literacy skills he possessed.

Through his work as a scribe, Ezra played a key role in preserving a post-exilic history of the Jewish people, but more importantly, Ezra eventually led a caravan of exiles back to Jerusalem, where he devoted his life to one message. He wanted everyone to heed the voice of God through the pages of His Word. Ezra's ministry of the Word would permeate his life to such a degree he would also organize the first order of Jewish scribes.[2] The Israelites had never imagined the destruction of the temple possible, which is why they scoffed at Jeremiah's earlier warnings.[3] But once the temple was destroyed and later rebuilt, Ezra knew they could never risk the possible destruction of the scrolls. So Ezra trained other priests to continue his work as a scribe, preserving God's Word by making meticulous copies of the scrolls.

Ezra was a Word Writer. And he invited others to join him in writing the Word.

The book of Ezra says,

> "Ezra had *determined* in his heart
> to *study* the law of the LORD, *obey* it,
> and *teach* its statutes and ordinances in Israel."
> —Ezra 7:10

In this verse we observe a sequence of four actionable steps,[4] and each part of this book is devoted to one step:

Part One—Determining in Your Heart

Ezra *determined* in his heart to make God's voice his guide. We'll follow Ezra from Babylon to Jerusalem and explore the obstacles that hindered the Israelites from

> Ezra was a Word Writer. And he invited others to join him in writing the Word.

choosing God's path. We'll find their obstacles are not so different from ours. I share my own story of spiritual exile and the reasons I determined in my heart that God's Word would be my soul's compass.

Part Two—To Study God's Word

Ezra knew he needed to *study* the law of the Lord to hear God's voice, and he called God's people to do the same. This call still sounds today. The ancient text of the Bible poses some challenges, but in Part Two we'll explore some of the moves we can make to help us overcome them.

> We're on a journey, not of perfection but of progression, to become more like Christ.

Part Three—To Obey God's Voice

Ezra purposed to *obey* what he read in Scripture. In the same way, we want to move the precepts we find in God's Word from our minds through our hearts to our hands. The goal is never mere accumulation of information, but rather spiritual transformation. We're on a journey, not of perfection but of progression, to become more like Christ.

Part Four—To Teach God's Precepts

Ezra yearned for God's people to do the same, so he sought to *teach* its statutes and ordinances. In the final chapters of this book, we'll dive deeper into "life after exile" and what it looks like to be stewards of the call on our lives.

As this book traces Ezra's journey from his exile in Babylon to his home in Jerusalem, I also share my own story of "going home." The most common motif in all of literature is the theme of "going home." Because something inside us knows we were made for something more than what we're experiencing here and now. Our souls long for something beyond what we can see and touch and hear and know. Apart from God, we're in a spiritual exile of our own, and our lives are a journey toward our true home. We're eternal souls living inside mortal bodies, and our physical world sometimes blinds us—and deafens us—from what is true versus what is untrue.

> God's Word is the only unchanging, eternal reality we can look to.

But you won't find any churchy clichés or perky platitudes here. Just an honest telling of a hard journey—hard in the way one wrestles with reconciling their theology with their reality.

In a world constantly spinning and a culture constantly changing, we all need something unchanging to hold on to—something steadfast to anchor our souls amidst the swirling turmoil around us and within us. God's Word is the only unchanging, eternal reality we can look to. Like the North Star pointing the way home for sailors who have no other fixed point to rely on, God's Word shows us the way home.

We don't have to be graduate students in seminary to be serious students of the Bible either. God's Word is just as much for the mom serving pizza to her kids in a living room as it is for the pastor serving on staff at a church. The Holy Spirit enables every believer, wherever we are, to understand the uncompromised truth and uncontested beauty of Scripture. When we hear God's voice through the pages of His Word, we find our true home in Him, and the brokenness we experience in the deep waters of life is redeemed for a purpose greater than we can imagine.

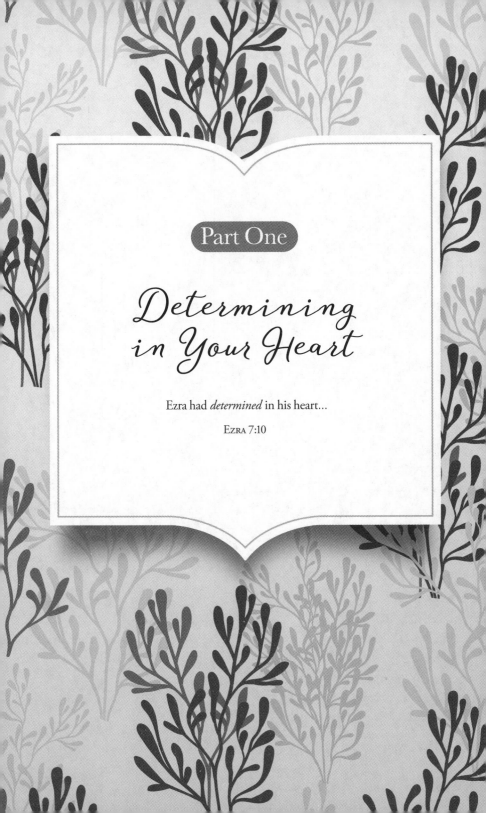

Part One

Determining in Your Heart

Ezra had *determined* in his heart...

EZRA 7:10

1

The Exile We Know

When they walk through the Valley of Weeping,
it will become a place of refreshing springs.

PSALM 84:6 NLT

California covers a vast territory. Mountains shrouded with evergreen. Beaches lined with sand. Forests impaled with redwood. At the heart of it all, like a spine connecting various parts of a body, a central valley stretches across a taut expanse of farmland. Here in the valley my hometown is like an island on a sea of rice fields. Flat terrain extends as far north and south as the eye permits. To the east and west, mountain ranges function like the sides of a canoe, while cement canals divide the land in between.

This is not the California everyone thinks of. Where men once rushed to find nuggets of gold lying in streams. Where celebrities have their names embossed in gold letters on sidewalks. Where a bridge is named the Golden Gate Bridge and the state flower is the golden poppy. Despite these iconic images, not everything here glitters with gold. The lesser-known heart of California is earthy and agrarian, a land where cows graze and farmers raise—chickens and pigs, bees and goats. This is where I'm from. A small, simple farming town called Willows. A town duly named, I'm told, for the weeping willows that sweep alongside the Sacramento River.

I'm from a place known for its weeping. The irony is not lost on me.

The chairs are all taken by adults, so I crouch in the corner of my brother's hospital room. Mom stands at the foot of his bed, her face wet with her own pain. The nurse behind a paper mask shoves a plastic tube several feet long through a hole in my brother's throat. His face contorts in agony. They've strapped his arms to the metal rails along the bed, but even with restraints it takes several nurses to hold him down. Despite his broken body, he's stronger than all of them.

When nobody's watching, I back out of the room and move in slow motion toward the window at the end of the hall. Pressing my forehead against the pane, I feel the condensation as drops of water form on the window, cold and damp. I envy the glass its ability to cry. For some reason what I feel inside can't make its way out, as though my tears are dammed as my headache worsens.

A timid hand touches my shoulder and I turn to see a nurse. Not from my brother's room but from a station down the hall. With nothing more than a soft look in her eye, she hands me a can of Sprite and slips away. I'm surprised she noticed me. For weeks now I've meandered through different parts of the hospital, wandering aimlessly about, figuring out which floors do what. I'm convinced I'm invisible.

At Grandma's house I saw *The Phantom of the Opera* on TV as a PBS special. As much as the show scared me, it mesmerized me. The phantom crept through secret tunnels, invisible to the rest of the world. That's how I feel now. Invisible. I'm here, but few people know, few people care. I slink down stairwells and edge past signs that say PERSONNEL ONLY. If someone in scrubs asks me how I got there, I feign innocence. Somehow I've gotten turned around, I explain, and I'm lost. The hospital worker kindly points me in the right direction then passes me by. Moments later I'm invisible again.

While roaming hospital floors, I discover a door with a placard that says CHAPEL. The room inside is smaller than my bedroom. It looks like a miniature sanctuary, complete with three tiny pews. Several symbols stretch across one wall. A cross. A crucifix. The Star of David. Plus a few others I don't recognize. It's a smorgasbord of religion.

Of all the symbols the crucifix draws my attention the most. I've never seen one so close. The crosses at my church are bare, but this one shows Jesus in 3-D. I touch the nails that perforate Jesus's hands and feet, and I think about the needles and tubes puncturing my brother's body. Pierced. His body broken. His blood spilled.

> The chapel becomes my sanctuary. My secret hiding place.

The chapel becomes my sanctuary. My secret hiding place. Whenever I need refuge from beeping machines and whispering adults, I come here to get away. Sometimes I lie on a pew with my knees dangling over the armrest and take a nap. Other times I finger through the pages of the huge Bible on the table at the front. But every page is filled with thees and thous. None of it makes sense.

Several times I try reading a tattered copy of *The Secret Garden* from my backpack. My sixth-grade book report is overdue, but I'm having a hard time concentrating because the opening pages are depressing. The protagonist in the story, a young girl, hides in corners while the plague sweeps through her home and village. She's surrounded by death.

Death surrounds me too, so I never leave this odd sanctuary without kneeling and praying the way I see grown-ups pray at church. I plead for God to end my brother's suffering. I try to bargain with Him too, but I don't have much to offer, just my bike and pup tent. So I beg, *Please, God, make his pain stop. Make him better or take him home.*

These, the only conceivable choices. But God doesn't answer either one of these prayers. My brother never makes it to heaven, although I'm told his heart stopped on the operating table. But he never gets better either. Instead, he's sentenced for life, imprisoned in a body that will never work right again.

Paralyzed.

Months later my brother Kendall comes home from the hospital. Our three-bedroom rental doesn't accommodate a wheelchair, and medical paraphernalia now fills every room. My two brothers always shared a bedroom and I had my own room, but we understand the need to give Kendall as much privacy as possible. So we move him into my bedroom.

Our house has a small laundry room in the back, except a twin-sized mattress won't fit in there, so Dad has some foam specially cut to make a bed for me in the nook by the washer and dryer. Between the wash cycle and spin cycle, I pull my copy of *The Secret Garden* from the small stack of books next to my makeshift bed. I failed my book report the year before; I never finished it. But something inside me wants to finish what I started before my brother's car accident—before a dark, pervasive sorrow consumed every aspect of our lives. I hated the book when I first tried to read it in the hospital, but this time it gives me hope.

The doctors say there's no hope of my brother ever walking again. In my book the main character arrives at her uncle's house and discovers a secret garden. Inside the secret garden her wheelchair-bound cousin can walk. Even though I know the story is fiction, I just have to believe something out there can make my brother walk again too. I have to find my own secret garden.

At first my hoped-for garden looks like possible surgeries or hopeful prayer meetings. My parents visit new doctors' offices in search of a cure. They call for prayer meetings at church and raise their hands toward heaven for a miracle. Then one day I watch my dad lift his 20-year-old son out of his wheelchair. He places his firstborn in the cab of his truck, and then folds the wheelchair and sets it in the back. Dad drives my brother to a Billy Graham Crusade.[1] So I stay up late because I want to celebrate with them when they return. I want to see my brother jump out of Dad's truck, shouting and praising God the way people in the Bible did when Jesus healed them.

Hours pass as the swoosh of the washer and the hum of the dryer woo me to sleep.

In the morning an eerie hush stifles the air. No one speaks. No one looks at each other. We shuffle to our cereal bowls, feeling the weight of this final blow. No surgery, no prayer meeting, and no super-evangelist can restore this brokenness.

Faith is crucified and buried.

Hope dies.

And a permanent wheelchair ramp is built to our front door.

My parents shutter the doors of the small church they lead. Faith is exiled to the past, while our new lives take on a lifelessness akin to my brother's dead legs. The prison of paralysis spreads to the heart. If we're supposed to walk by faith, we'd settle just for walking.

I give up on ever finding a magical garden.

> I can't write a book about how life-changing the Bible is without also sharing my struggle to believe everything the Bible says.

I can't write a book about the Bible, telling you how life-changing it is—no matter how true that truth is—without also sharing my struggle to believe everything the Bible says. That God is good. That He cares about our tears. That we can trust Him with our bodies and our lives. I've especially struggled with verses like Jeremiah 29:11 that talk about God's plans to prosper us and not to harm us.

Tell that to my brother.

Tell that to the mom with stage 4 breast cancer.

Tell that to the child who's just lost a mom or dad or both.

Nevertheless, Jeremiah 29:11 remains a favorite verse for many:

> "'I know the plans I have for you,' declares the LORD, 'plans to prosper you and not to harm you, plans to give you hope and a future'" (NIV).

This sounds like a great promise—plans filled with hope and a future that looks bright. It sounds awfully close to the idealized American Dream with its inherent promise of life, liberty, and the pursuit of happiness. No wonder we westerners love Jeremiah 29:11 so much. It's the perfect Bible verse for a meme on Instagram or Facebook. But what about the rest of Jeremiah's book?

> *Jeremiah 29:11 is the perfect Bible verse for a meme on Instagram or Facebook. But what about the rest of Jeremiah's book?*

When we zoom in a little closer to see what is really happening in the world of the Jews when Jeremiah prophesies those now-popular words, we see a nation near extinction, a people condemned to utter degradation. Starved. Murdered. Captured. Enslaved. Exiled. If news cameras had been around, footage would have shown dead bodies, both large and small, lying in dirt streets with vultures prey-ing on human flesh. The survivors were forced to march across a desert, live in a foreign land, learn a new language, and serve the very people who had killed their families and their entire way of life.

What about those plans to prosper them? And not to harm them? What kind of hope and future could they possibly have in Babylon?

The horror the Hebrews experienced when the Babylonians invaded Jerusalem was a holocaust before the Holocaust. And it's to these survivors Jeremiah speaks, "I know the plans I have for you…" The "you" here is plural. Jeremiah isn't speaking to an indi-vidual. He's speaking to a community that has just experienced the worst thing any community could possibly endure. God promises to bring His people back to Jerusalem in 70 years. God promises to restore their former way of life. And ultimately, God promises to send a Savior—a King who will vanquish their enemy.

God makes good on His promise too. Decades later the Per-sians defeat the Babylonians, and a new king—a Mr. Cyrus of Per-sia—makes a royal decree. The Hebrews can go home, and the new government in power will pay the cost to rebuild their temple in Jerusalem.

Such a turn of events.

Around 50,000 Hebrews choose to make the 900-mile trek back across the desert.[2] This was a scant portion of the Hebrew popula-tion living in Babylon at the time. The majority of the Hebrews had assimilated into their new country, and they preferred to stay put.

Years pass. Another king takes over. And it's here in Babylon we find Ezra, a Levite in captivity. In Babylon, Aramaic is the language of the day, but Ezra is fluent in Hebrew as well. His exceptional lit-eracy skills garner him a prestigious post in Babylonian government. He has access to legal documents, as well as the new king, Artaxerxes.

But something stirs deep inside Ezra when he hears the news of the rebuilt temple in Jerusalem. With the temple restored, his heritage as a priest is also restored, so Ezra approaches the king and seeks permission to return to Jerusalem. The king not only agrees to let Ezra go, but also grants him everything he requests. [3]

The Hebrews in Babylon lived in literal exile, but their lives exemplify the spiritual exile we all experience apart from God.

With this second caravan, only 1500 Hebrews choose to return with Ezra. Again, the majority wish to remain in Babylon. I can't judge them, though, for their desire to stay speaks to the condition of a soul in captivity. The longer we live in captivity, the more accustomed we grow to it and the harder it becomes to break free from bondage and embrace true freedom. Maybe some of them wanted to return to Jerusalem, but the four-month hike through a perilous desert seemed too much to bear. Or maybe they'd simply grown comfortable where they were. Assimilation, for many, was complete. Most of the younger generation couldn't even understand the Hebrew language anymore. Why risk the journey for an unknown land with an unknown language?

The Hebrews in Babylon lived in literal exile, but their lives exemplify the spiritual exile we all experience apart from God. And everyone's spiritual exile looks different. For some, spiritual exile may look like rebellion against parental expectations and traditional norms. For many, spiritual exile can look like hardworking folks simply going about their daily lives, trying to earn a living, but doing so with a dogged determination of self-reliance. For me, spiritual exile looked more like bewildered confusion, feeling abandoned by God. While other families still dressed in their Sunday best trotted off to church in station wagons, my brother struggled with doorways too narrow for a wheelchair and wooden cabinets under sinks that prevented access for something as routine as brushing your teeth.

Thirty years later our lives remain split between the before and after. Life before the car accident. And life after the car accident. This same phenomenon reverberates throughout history and across geography. Life before the cancer. Life after the cancer. Life before 9-11. Life after. Life before Hurricane Katrina. Life after.

The way lightning from heaven splits a tree to its core, calamity separates time. Our lives become forever oriented to its strike, and the brokenness in its wake leaves us reeling, not knowing how to move forward. More often than not these experiences define our being, shaping—or misshaping—our views about God and prayer and faith and hope, rendering the broken ever more broken. But when the deep waters of suffering threaten to take the very breath right out of us, the deeper waters of life with God speak hope into the impossible.

> With a broken body God restored humanity's brokenness.

For years too long I believed a broken body broke my family. I couldn't fathom how a broken body could be used to restore wholeness and peace where strife had rent asunder the life-beating soul of father and mother, brother and sister. Yet that is exactly what happened when heaven opened and sent Light into the world, separating time between BC and AD. Thirty years upon this earth, Jesus built with carpenter's hands and helped with younger siblings. This the before. Then the unthinkable.

Soldiers surrounded Him and stretched out His arms. They nailed His hands and feet to splintered crossbeams while onlookers stood nearby, hurling insults and mocking His name.

Jesus was crucified and buried.

Hope died.

Then hope came back to life.

With a broken body God restored humanity's brokenness. Now the scarred hands of the One and Only hold the one and only promise of wholeness. And the King is extending an invitation—today, right now, this very moment—for every spiritual exile to return to his or her true home in Him, where a person's core identity is restored and divine purpose is fulfilled.

2

The Lament We Feel

I will never forget this awful time, as I grieve over my loss.
Yet I still dare to hope when I remember this:
The faithful love of the LORD never ends! His mercies never cease.

LAMENTATIONS 3:20-22 NLT

My earliest memory is on stage at church. While Dad worked in the church office, I'd drag the drummer's stool over to the pulpit, climb onto the wobbling seat, and tap the microphone to pretend to see if it was really on—the same way I watched Dad tap it on Sunday mornings. I played church. Preaching to my imaginary congregation. Collecting the offering plates. Passing out communion trays.

The pulpit stood between two altars. My parents loved to tell people how their oldest son made those altars in woodshop at school. They were long and smooth and stained dark walnut. On Sunday mornings a church service rarely ended without an invitation to come to the altar, ushering in a few moments of solemnity. Quiet. Serene. Then after a brief time of silence, Mom began to sing. The congregation soon joined her.

I loved singing worship choruses and hymns. While playing church on weekday mornings, I knelt at the altar last, with the same reverence I observed on Sundays, and I sang the songs I knew by heart. Whenever I sang, alone at the altar, I sensed something I couldn't articulate. I experienced a peace and a wholeness I couldn't describe.

God's presence. Real and palpable.

No playmaking. No pretending.

So when I found myself kneeling at an altar in a hospital chapel, I sang there too. But only at first.

A week after my brother's car accident, Mom calls one of her sisters from a payphone. Our hometown is too small for a hospital, so we're staying in an old Victorian house across the street from this big-city hospital. My parents can't go home for a change of clothes. They take turns sleeping in a chair by my brother's bed because they want to be there to say good-bye if he doesn't make it. So Mom asks her sister if she could pick me up and take me home. I'd been sleeping on a roll-away bed for several days in the same clothes.

The drive from our little town to the city is 35 miles of country roads that zigzag through orchards and fields. No freeway provides direct access, and most folks only make the trip to the city every once in a while. When my aunt arrives, she doesn't seem happy. This extra trip for me is clearly an inconvenience for her, and she doesn't speak to me the entire drive home. When she pulls into our driveway, she doesn't turn off the engine. Her only words, "You got a key?"

I nod, say thank you for bringing me home, and climb out of her car. My aunt is gone before I reach the door.

As I step inside I crinkle my nose. The emptiness of the house is punctuated by the kind of staleness that proves no one has been here for days. Everything appears the same, but somehow different at the same time. I call for my bird—a sweet little canary the color of butter, with wing tips that look as though she dipped the ends of her feathers in turquoise paint. I try to imitate her morning song to solicit her response, but when I reach my bedroom, fear strikes me cold as I rush to the empty cage. How could she get out while I was gone?

But she isn't gone. She's lying at the bottom of her cage. Very still. I open the ivory metal door and scoop her into my shaking palm. So stiff. But her feathers as soft as ever. I whisper, "Wake up. Please, wake up." I can't understand how this has happened. "God, please make her wake up!"

I notice her bowl is empty. Her water bottle dry. How many days has it been? How long have I been gone?

I sit on my bed for a long time holding her. I tell her, over and over, "I'm sorry, so sorry, I didn't mean to, please forgive me, I'm so sorry." The sinking sun casts long shadows through my window. I don't know what else to do, so I carry my song-less bird to the back-yard and kneel beneath my favorite willow. I lay her next to me while I dig through the dirt with my hands.

I want to cry. I know I would feel better if I could just get the tears to come, but something is wrong with my tear ducts. I'm sure of it. Why can't I cry?

I place her deep into the ground and stare at her. She's not in pain anymore. Her suffering is over. Something inside me wants to make the hole bigger so I can climb inside too. Perhaps death is the answer to all suffering and pain.

With fistfuls of dirt I sprinkle fine crumbs of dust over my feathered friend until I can't see her anymore.

The next five years feel like someone took the deck of cards we called our life and reshuffled everything. My parents divorce and then move to new cities with new spouses and new lives. My two brothers, now well beyond high school, have moved into their own apartment. Kendall can use his arms, so he's amazingly independent, considering his many limitations in a wheelchair. At home, it's just Mom and me and my new stepdad. We've moved to Sacramento, and my powers of hiding are no longer necessary since my new high school has more than 2000 students—roughly half the size of the town I grew up in. Anonymity here is easy, and I never tell anyone the thoughts that plague me. Thoughts of fresh dirt and the pain ceasing with an endless sleep beneath a willow tree.

Sitting at the kitchen table, I trace the edge of the blue checkered tablecloth with my index finger while Mom dries the dishes. Something's been gnawing at me and I'm not sure how to talk about it. Dad changed. He grew a beard and started smoking. And when he left town, he left church too, for the same reason I suppose a lot of people give up on church and the idea of a benevolent God—because they believe God abandoned them in their darkest hour. Didn't Jesus confirm as much? While hanging on the cross, He uttered the most painful words ever spoken: "My God, My God, why have You forsaken Me?"[1]

So why is it different for Mom? Kendall is her son too. Doesn't she feel abandoned by God? After everything that's happened, why is she okay when nothing else is?

"Mom, why do you still go to church?"

She sets the dish towel aside and looks out the kitchen window, as if seeing something beyond the horizon. She answers me with three seemingly random questions.

"Denise, do you know what the shortest verse in the Bible is?"

"Yeah, whenever the youth pastor asks us if we've memorized any Bible verses that week, some kids start shouting, 'Jesus wept!'"

Mom nods and then changes the subject. "Did you know those little numbers in the Bible that separate chapters and verses aren't in the original manuscripts? They were added years later for easier reference."

No, I didn't know that.

Then Mom looks at me and says, "You know how a complete sentence needs both a subject and a predicate?"

Yes, I do know this. But what does grammar have to do with anything? I try not to roll my eyes.

"Well," she says, "the subject of the shortest verse in the Bible could have been about anybody—like Abraham or Moses or David or Paul. But, of course, it's about Jesus. And the predicate of the shortest verse in the Bible could have showed Jesus doing any number of things. It could have said 'Jesus prayed' or 'Jesus healed' or 'Jesus smiled.'"

> Our time of weeping, our time of suffering— though it may last a lifetime, it is bound by time.

Her eyes turn back to the window, her gaze steady before continuing, "I don't think it's a coincidence that when the scribes assigned numbers for chapters and verses, the shortest verse in the Bible says 'Jesus wept.' I think it's just one more way God is communicating to all of us that our time of weeping, our time of suffering— your brother's suffering—though it may last a lifetime, it is bound by time. And just as that one small verse is so short when compared to the rest of the Bible, all human suffering will one day, as hard as it is to imagine now, seem so short when compared to all of eternity."

Silence settles in the kitchen until the teakettle bubbles to a whistle. Mom slips her hand into a gloved pot holder and pours hot water into a teapot while I think about eternity and everything I've always heard about heaven. A place where all tears are supposedly erased and all pain has ceased. I want to ask another question, but I'm afraid to admit the idea of a blissful heaven after this life sounds like something someone made up to help us feel better when we're hurting. I'm not sure I buy the whole heaven thing. But I do get how Jesus could cry out, "My God, My God, why have You forsaken Me?"

Yeah, I get that.

3

The Decision We Make

*The LORD said, "Go out and stand on the mountain
in the presence of the LORD, for the LORD is about to pass by."*

1 KINGS 19:11 NIV

A new friend at school invites me to church and I learn it's within walking distance of my house, so the following Sunday I walk to church by myself. It's easily the largest church I've ever been to. At least a hundred people wear choir robes and sing on stage, but the service feels surprisingly familiar, just on a larger scale. I always loved singing at church, especially the old hymns. The peace and wholeness I experienced during worship as a kid—that presence I couldn't put into words—is here in this mega-sized church.

> Could I really bring my pain to the One who allowed so much of it in the first place?

Scouring the bulletin, I see an announcement for summer camp, and weeks later I pile into a van with other teenagers. We ride for hours to a rustic campground in the highlands. When you live in the valley, any trip to the mountains is an adventure. The landscape is different. The evergreens shower the earth with pine needles and blanket the ground with much-needed respites of shade. Streams of water flow through natural crevices of rock rather than irrigation ditches.

Here, too, something I can't explain transpires during the worship songs. It's like going back in time to a place that felt safe, secure. My eyes leak against my will, and I'm not sure why. Why here? Why now? I'd long since grown accustomed to the weight of an everyday heaviness. My desire to cry left me a long time ago. I accepted the heaviness I felt as part of my new normal. Besides, could I really bring my pain to the One who allowed so much of it in the first place? Part of me thinks I could. Part of me thinks I shouldn't. So I fight it. After willing myself to cry for so many years and failing, I now will myself not to.

At the end of a morning message, the speaker asks us to spend the next 20 minutes alone—reading our Bible. I've never actually read my Bible. The truth is, my Bible embarrasses me. The letters *NIV* stand tall on the binding, but the cover shows a cartoonish picture of Jesus with little kids on His lap. It looks like a kiddie Bible, and I've been hiding it from my new friends all week.

I meander a bit until I happen upon a path that leads uphill. I hike for more than 20 minutes, and I'm certain everyone down the hill is already finished reading. Only I haven't even begun, and now I'm curious where this trail will lead.

The incline eventually levels out and the trail spills into a meadow covered in wild grass. Tall pine trees stand as sentinels around the circumference, guarding this hidden sanctuary in nature. A fallen timber invites me to kneel, like an altar waiting. So I place my Bible on top of the log and fumble with its pages, unsure where to begin.

The Table of Contents leads me to the "New" part of the Bible, but I skim past the genealogy in the first chapter of Matthew to read the familiar story of Mary and baby Jesus. But I'm aghast at the part where King Herod ordered all the boys under two years of age to be murdered. Why did Christ's arrival begin with pain? Why did those poor parents have to watch soldiers burst through their front doors and kill their sons? Why must parents watch their children suffer at all? I think of my own mom and dad, and I can't shake the injustice of it all. It's not right. I can't reconcile it.

I give up on Matthew.

I flip and skip until I land in the book of James. A different font on the page explains that James is the younger brother of Jesus. Instantly I feel a kinship with James; he's the sibling of suffering. James understands. He had an older brother who was tortured and crucified.

In chapter 2 a verse stops me cold. James says the demons believe in God.[1] I only know two verses in the Bible by heart, "Jesus wept" and John 3:16, which says whoever believes in Jesus will have eternal life. Except that seems to contradict what James says, because surely the demons won't be in heaven—not if it's supposed to be a place without pain.

> When I'm tempted to question whether God is real or not real, I always come back to this: I believe in right and wrong.

I've always believed in God. To me the existence of God is as obvious as the wind. On days when I'm tempted to question it all, whether He's real or not real, I always come back to this: I believe in right and wrong. I believe it was wrong of King Herod to send soldiers into people's homes to kill innocent babies and toddlers. I believe it's wrong when someone takes something that doesn't belong to them. I believe it's wrong to make a promise and not keep it.

In science class at school we're told we come from some primordial soup. That we're nothing more than an accumulation of chemical reactions, evolving into more sophisticated homo sapiens. Illustrations in my textbook show apes growing taller and leaner until a man is standing on the right. We're told all of evolution is based on the survival of the fittest. If that were true, we'd be okay with soldiers barging into homes at night killing baby boys because those soldiers were obviously fitter than infants.

But it's not true. And common sense knows it.

> The basic fact there's a right and a wrong means something is placed inside us to know the difference.

If we're nothing more than evolved beings, then we have no grounds for condemning the actions of murder and rape and theft and deception. In evolutionary terms, the strong have an inherent mandate to overpower the weak. But that's nonsense. When the mighty conquer the needy, nothing but chaos ensues. The basic fact there's a right and a wrong means something is placed inside us to know the difference. Some call it a conscience, but I've always believed that thing inside us, whatever we call it, was placed there by something—or Someone—and it draws us to that which is good and beautiful and true.

I've never struggled to believe God is real, but I've struggled mightily to believe He is trustworthy. When the youth group circles up by the vans to pray for "traveling mercies," I wince inwardly and question immediately. How come God didn't provide traveling mercies for my brother? How can I ever trust Him to keep me safe? This question burrows beneath the surface of my everyday interactions. I don't feel safe. Every car ride to school or the grocery store or even to church feels dangerous. I can't trust God to keep me safe, because He didn't keep my brother safe. Nothing feels safe to me. My family doesn't feel safe. My future doesn't feel safe. My own body doesn't feel safe.

I believe God is real because I could never believe the "survival of the fittest" is right or good or true, but everything inside me resists the notion that I can trust God. That He is good. Not that He is bad, just indifferent. I'm not convinced He cares.

Then I read in James that even the demons believe in God. The demons? The angels who left God's presence to pursue their own gain? There must be something more to this "believing" than mere intellectual assent. What else am I supposed to believe? I want to feel safe. I want to trust. But I'm afraid. Deeply afraid. Especially of the darkness that hovers over the door of my heart, trying to get in, wanting to swallow me in a grave. I know that is real too.

A word comes to mind: *surrender*.

Is there a difference between believing there is a God and surrendering my life to Him?

I know the answer even as I ask it, and I can't help but wonder if this difference makes all the difference in the world, both here and beyond. So I ask Him, *God, show me what it means to live in such a way that it's more than just believing about You. I want to trust You, but I don't know how. Help me learn to trust You.*

My eyes start leaking again. I sense the same presence here at nature's altar as when I knelt at the altar my brother made with his hands, back when his feet still ran and jumped and skipped.

A deep peace envelops me, and that other feeling—the one that wishes I could crawl inside the dirt, the one that dreams of ways to fall into a never-ending sleep, the one always accompanied by a heavy weight on my chest and shoulders—leaves.

> If God could use the people in Genesis, maybe He can use me too.

I have no words for what is happening. All I know is this heaviness that's been with me for years is gone. So I keep reading the Bible, and with each page I turn a new desire consumes me, a desire to read more. I have this desire to return to the beginning. I must start with Genesis and work my way back to James, without skipping anything. I must know who this God is—a God who whispers hope into the hidden heart of a lonely girl.

I return home from camp and start at the beginning, in Genesis, and I make the most startling discovery. Those people from Sunday school stories—Abraham, Isaac, and Jacob—they're all related. They're grandfather, father, and son. Perhaps there's something to those boring genealogies after all.

I find the book of Genesis strangely comforting, too, because the people in those stories were a mess. Yet God chose to use them? If God could use them, maybe He could use me too. Because I know a thing or two about coming from a family that's a bit of a mess.

My journey through the Old Testament continues with as many revelations as newfound confusions. After 70 years of exile in Babylon, the first caravan of exiles return to Jerusalem to rebuild the temple. Ezra arrives in Jerusalem with the second caravan. His heritage designates him a priest, so he assumes his new role. In a special dedication of the temple, Ezra reads the book of the Law to the people.[2] They stand to hear God's Word read to them. They stand for hours! Their posture conveys not only reverence, but also a deep thirst for God's Word. Many returnees couldn't speak Hebrew anymore, not after growing up in Babylon. So Ezra had 13 Levites stand throughout the crowd, and they interpreted and explained in Aramaic what Ezra read in Hebrew.[3]

I wish I had someone like that now. Someone who could explain the parts of the Bible that confuse me. Thankfully, reading through the Psalms is a more pleasant experience, until I read the first verse in Psalm 22: "My God, My God, why have You forsaken Me?"

Wait a minute. These are the words of Jesus. I haven't come to the Gospels yet, but I've heard plenty of sermons about Jesus hanging on the cross, crying out against God for abandoning Him. But here in Psalm 22 we find the same words, which means when Jesus spoke them, He was quoting Scripture. So in the worst moment of His life, when His body is racked with excruciating pain and the sins of the world are heaped upon Him, Jesus takes the time to recite a psalm? Why? Was He really feeling abandoned by God? Or was He communicating something else?

These words penned by David describe the lament of the suffering innocent. The first part of Psalm 22 decries the harsh reality of someone suffering unjustly. This is the before. Then the after. The second part of Psalm 22 decrees the wonder of restoration. By psalm's end, there's a great turning. The conditions of the afflicted are reversed. Their suffering is over. Their empty stomachs are filled. Their hearts are given eternal life. And their redemption shall be told to future generations.

> Jesus preached the most powerful sermon in the history of the world in just nine words.

Jesus's mother, Mary; His disciple, John; and all the Pharisees and other Hebrews standing near the cross knew their Scriptures. When they heard Jesus quote Psalm 22:1, they would have recognized the entire theme of that psalm. It's as if Jesus was telling everyone, "You know how Psalm 22 ends. That's how this is going to end too."

Yes, God turned His face from the sin Jesus became for our sakes, but Jesus knew that moment would split time in two, leading to something whole and new. When Jesus recited Psalm 22:1, He preached the most powerful sermon in the history of the world in just nine words. Every Hebrew standing within earshot of the cross knew how Psalm 22 ends—"People not yet born will be told: 'The LORD saved his people'" (Psalm 22:31 GNT).

The Lord saved His people. That's how Psalm 22 ends.

It's just one more way God is communicating to all of us that He knows how things are going to end. And the ending is a good one. Our suffering, here and now, will end. My brother's suffering will end.

My mom is right. One day, all human suffering will seem so short when compared to all of eternity. There's a life beyond this life. It's the life for which Jesus prepared a way for us to enter.

I believe.

4

The Challenges We Face

He sent His word and healed them...

PSALM 107:20

Sitting in the hospital chapel, I search my backpack for something to do. Even though I already know what's inside, I dig through each zippered pocket, hoping to find inspiration. I decide on my notebook and open it to the first blank page. Near the top I write *Dear Diary*. I've never been a diary keeper, but I don't know how many hours I'll be in the hospital today. I figure I might as well spend the time writing. Except *Diary* isn't a real person, so I feel stymied.

Swinging my feet beneath the pew, I look around the chapel and see the now-familiar crucifix on the wall. I scratch out ~~Diary~~ and write *Jesus*. With a real person to write to, the words pour onto the page. I tell Jesus everything that's been happening. Somehow the simple act of telling Jesus about my day makes the day seem a little lighter.

When the hospital days end, I don't have as much time to write. I'm back at school and behind on my schoolwork. I stop talking to Jesus with words on paper. But years later, when I return home from camp and begin reading my Bible, I pull out a notebook

> This prayer becomes the cry of my heart: *Speak, for Your servant is listening.*

43

again, this time to write down my favorite verses, and sometimes entire psalms.

My favorite stories include the ark of the covenant, God's holy dwelling place. I love how the boy Samuel slept in the temple, not far from the ark. I want to be close to God's presence like that. When Samuel hears God's voice, he thinks the priest is calling him. But the priest eventually figures out God is speaking to Samuel and he gives the best advice ever. He tells Samuel to respond to God by saying, "Speak, for Your servant is listening."[1]

This prayer becomes the cry of my heart. I pray it throughout my day, especially when I sit down to read my Bible. *Speak, for Your servant is listening.* I write these words in my notebook.

But there's another story about the ark of the covenant that bothers me. After David becomes king, he wants to bring the ark to Jerusalem. His troops place it on a cart to transport it with oxen. At one point an ox stumbles and the ark is about to fall to the ground, so a guy named Uzzah reaches out to grab it. He prevents the ark from touching the ground, and then something like lightning from heaven strikes him dead right there on the spot.

He was just trying to help!

This story doesn't jive with other places in the Bible that say God is merciful and kind and full of grace. So I grab the Yellow Pages and look up the address to a nearby Christian bookstore. I'm certain I need a different Bible. One that comes with explanations. Because I need to know why a loving God would kill Uzzah.

At the bookstore I'm overwhelmed by the choices. Combinations of capital letters confuse me: KJV, NIV, NASB, and so many more. A wrinkly lady with bright red lipstick offers to help me pick one.

"Hi. I'm looking for a new Bible," I explain. "The kind with answers."

She smiles. "The Bible has all the answers you'll ever need, sweetie."

"Is there a Bible with explanations? Like why God killed Uzzah?"

The wrinkles on her forehead increase. "Oh, perhaps you're looking for a study Bible," she says. "They have the biblical text at the top with descriptions and explanations at the bottom." She selects a box from the shelf behind her and shows me the inside of a study Bible.

My eyes widen as I point to the words at the bottom half of the page. "Are those like CliffsNotes? Yes! That's exactly what I need."

To my delight, I discover real grown-up Bibles come in pink faux leather, and I rush home to read the bottom half of my new Bible.

To my dismay, the bottom half doesn't tell me why God killed Uzzah. It gives me a list of other passages. Most regrettably the list sends me back to Numbers and Leviticus—the very parts of the Bible I had hoped to never return to. Once through was enough, thank you. But I'm kind of mad about Uzzah. I can't shake it. It seems unfair. So I go back and read the verses listed in the bottom half of my Bible. In Numbers 4:15, the Lord gives specific instructions to Moses and his brother, Aaron.

> After Aaron and his sons have finished covering the holy furnishings and all the holy articles, and when the camp is ready to move, only then are the Kohathites to come and do the carrying. But they must not touch the holy things or they will die. The Kohathites are to carry those things that are in the tent of meeting (NIV).

Two things become immediately clear. First, Uzzah wasn't a Kohathite, so he wasn't following the Lord's instructions. His disobedience cost him his life. Still, punishment by death seems harsh. How about a little grace? Then the second thing: the word *holy* is mentioned three times in this one verse. The holy furnishings. The holy articles. The holy things.

The ark of the covenant was holy because it was God's dwelling place, and God is holy.

As I read the other passages listed at the bottom of my Bible, a new picture comes into focus. In Leviticus 10:1-2, Aaron's two sons violate God's instructions and they're also killed immediately. Again, it's a disobedience thing, but the punishment still seems disproportionate to the offense. Then I read the next verse.

> Moses then said to Aaron, "This is what the LORD spoke of when he said: 'Among those who approach me I will be proved holy; in the sight of all the people I will be honored'" (Leviticus 10:3 NIV).

The story of Uzzah shows us what we deserve: death. It also shows us whom we need: Jesus.

There it is again. That word *holy*. The Lord is holy. So holy, in fact, that no one can approach Him. No one. This is the result of Adam and Eve's disobedience. God expelled them from the garden of Eden not to be mean, but because they could no longer be in the presence of His holiness. At least not without a sacrifice to atone for their sins.

All those animal sacrifices in the Old Testament? They foreshadow the ultimate sacrifice in the person of Jesus. Because of Jesus and His sacrifice on the cross, we no longer have to fear the presence of His holiness.

What happened to Uzzah is what should happen to *all* of us because our sin separates us from God's holy presence. The story of Uzzah is a real-life illustration. It shows us what we deserve: death. It also shows us whom we need: Jesus. Without Jesus we cannot enter into God's presence, because He is holy.

Now I'm reading the Bible with new eyes. I'm no longer skimming the boring parts and looking for the interesting parts. I'm looking for the way each story illustrates some aspect of God's character. The story of Uzzah points to God's character as holy and to our need for Jesus. This is the central story of the whole Bible.

The time I spend reading and writing the words of Scripture reshapes me. More than anything a deep thirst to know more, to understand more, grows inside me. I finish my senior year of high school and continue to visit the aisles of the Christian bookstore often. I want to hear from other people who have experienced what I've been experiencing. I find them too. In books by C.S. Lewis and Dietrich Bonhoeffer and others. Their stories fascinate me. God has been changing the lives of men and women well beyond biblical times. And there's a common thread among every one of these life changes: the Bible. People have been hearing God's voice through the pages of the Bible for centuries, and He's still speaking through His Word today.

> God has been changing lives well beyond biblical times. And there's a common thread among every one: the Bible.

With my love of words and books, I study literature and composition in college and become an English teacher. I love teaching books, but there's only one Book with living words. It's my favorite book to teach.

My students find their seats while I take a blue dry-erase marker and scrawl the daily writing prompt on the white board: *Why is the Bible boring?* The chatter that normally accompanies the first few minutes of class instantly quiets down, and I notice a few students tilting their heads sideways, as if a different angle will reveal a hidden meaning.

I know what they're thinking: *This must be a trick question.*

No one responds and the unspoken taboo is clear. We're not supposed to call the Bible boring. This is a Christian university, after all; it's customary to discuss the Bible as both ancient literature and the infallible Word of God, so it must seem near-blasphemous for their English professor to insinuate the Bible is boring.

I rewrite the question: *Why do some people consider the Bible boring?* This is safer, for it relocates the presumed boredom on other people. Surely none of us in the room have ever encountered a dry passage of Scripture.

A brave young woman raises a lone hand. "I think some people consider the Bible boring because it was written a long time ago in another language, which makes it hard to understand."

"You're absolutely right," I say. "The original text is written in other languages. So unless we learn Greek and Hebrew and a little Aramaic, we're left with a variety of English translations to choose from."

Another hand goes up. This time a young man interjects, "Some people consider the Bible boring because our world is different now. It's hard to relate."

I nod as a few more hands go up, and I begin a list on the board: *ancient language, different culture.*

A student from the back of the room says, "Genealogies are the worst."

Someone else counters, "No, the laws about cows and donkeys are the worst. None of it pertains to us."

I add *boring genealogies* and *outdated laws* to my growing list while another student chimes in with a rather literary observation.

"The Bible is boring because it doesn't read like a real book. It doesn't follow the normal pattern of exposition, conflict, rising action, climax, and resolution."

I can't help but smile. "That's true. The Bible doesn't appear to be arranged in the normal pattern stories typically follow." I write *lack of flow* on the board.

My quietest student now joins the conversation and says, "When I read the Bible, I can't always tell when what I'm reading is supposed to be a metaphor or if it's meant to be literal."

A general murmur of consensus follows as I write *confusing metaphors*. Then I walk around the tables until I'm standing at the back of the room, facing the whiteboard like my students. Together we stare at the list we've compiled:

- ancient language
- different culture
- outdated laws
- boring genealogies
- lack of flow
- confusing metaphors

"I'm sure we could add more," I say, "but this is a good start. When I read the Bible for the first time, I felt the same way."

I make my way back to the front of the classroom and tell the same story I've told all my students. When I was in high school, I went to camp. The speaker challenged us to read the Bible for 20 minutes. Parts of it were, indeed, boring and confusing. But then...

I pause from telling my story and look at each of my students' faces. It's one of those rare moments when no one's distracted by a cell phone, and I realize no one has ever given them permission to call certain parts of the Bible confusing, much less boring. What's more, many of them heard the same stories in Sunday school I heard growing up, but they're unable to piece together the overarching story that's woven throughout the Old and New Testaments.

My students are right to point out the apparent *lack of flow*. While some parts of the Bible flow, other parts seem like detours from the story. They don't flow at all. Not only that, but the arrangement of the Bible doesn't follow the chronological order of events. Add to that the cultural differences between biblical times and today's society and it's no wonder the Bible seems so confusing.

> The more time we spend in the Bible, the more familiar we become with God's voice.

Despite these very real challenges, the Bible does become clearer with time. And that's what Part Two of this book is devoted to—equipping you with the tools you need for accessing the language of the Bible to discern its meaning, apply its truth, and, most importantly, know God in a deeper way. That's why we read the Bible. To know God and the purpose to which He has called us.

God isn't a silent God. He speaks to us through His Word. The more time we spend in the Bible, the more familiar we become with His voice, making it easier to recognize it when He speaks. The prayer I started praying as a teenager in high school is the same prayer I pray today, and it's a prayer I encourage you to make your own as well: *Speak, for Your servant is listening.*

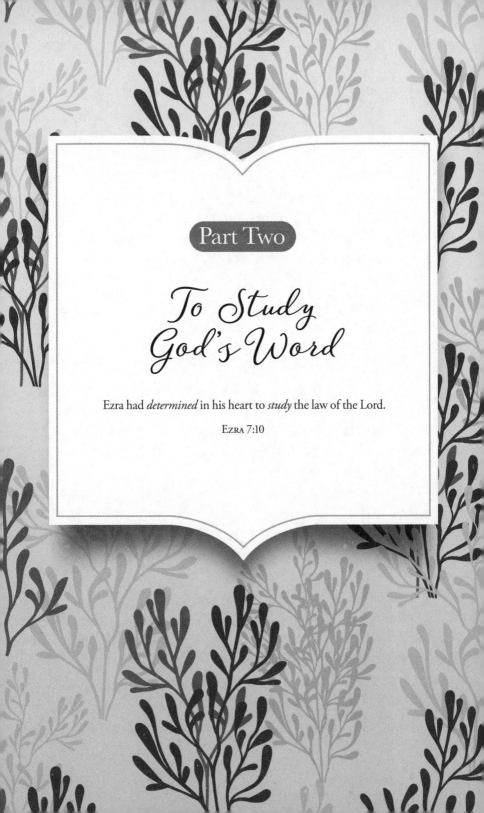

Part Two

To Study God's Word

Ezra had *determined* in his heart to *study* the law of the Lord.

EZRA 7:10

5

The Water We Need

Come, everyone who is thirsty, come to the waters.

Isaiah 55:1

The 35-mile drive from the hospital to our house—from the city to our small town—is like a well-worn path. I don't know the names of the roads, but I know every turn. First, it's the almond orchards, then the willow trees. I know when the river is close because we pass under two distinct willows. Their long, sinewy leaves hang over the road, but someone has cut them at a straight horizontal angle so cars can pass underneath, untouched. The poor willows look like my bangs when Mom stretches Scotch Tape across the hair on my forehead to help her cut a straight line.

Past the badly cut willow trees, we come to the river. I like to lean against the car window and watch the water rushing beneath the bridge. To one side is a clearing with a few picnic tables. Our church comes here for the annual summer potluck. We eat cold fried chicken, play croquet, and finish the day with baptisms in the river. My dad baptized me here, back when faith was sweet and the only crosses I'd seen were two simple beams.

Why We Need the Word Every Day

No matter how many years pass, whenever I return home to the valley, I drive to the river, to the place between city and town, for I'll always feel like a part of me is in both—the small town and the big city.

The Sacramento River splits the valley lengthwise, providing much-needed irrigation for the many rice fields blanketing the natural floodplain. Compared to the Nile, the Sacramento is a mere sliver of water, winding through the valley. Yet I marvel at its impact on life. Without water, nothing grows. So it's not surprising that God likens His Word to water. The prophet Isaiah said,

> For as the rain and the snow come down from heaven and do not return there but water the earth, making it bring forth and sprout, giving seed to the sower and bread to the eater, so shall my word be that goes out from my mouth (Isaiah 55:10-11 esv).

> Just as water sustains physical life, God's Word sustains spiritual life.

Consider the image of rain and snow—falling from heaven, watering the earth. We can last a few weeks without food, but we'll last a scant few days without water. Water is the most basic physical need we have, so it's no wonder God says His Word is like water. Just as water sustains physical life, God's Word sustains spiritual life. For health and vitality, both are needed daily. God made it that way.

We need water, not only for nourishment but also for cleansing. When the exiles returned from Babylon, they commenced the reconstruction of Jerusalem—the temple, the city, and the city's walls. Once restored, the people came together to hear Ezra the priest read from the book of the Law.

So Ezra the priest brought the Law before the assembly,
both men and women...And he read from it facing the
square before the Water Gate from early morning until
midday (Nehemiah 8:2-3 ESV).

Ezra stood at the Water Gate to share
God's Word. In ancient Jerusalem, the Water
Gate was the place where people drew water
for bathing. Here again the Word of God is
tied to the symbol of water. As Ezra gave the
Word, the imagery of water pouring forth
to clean the whole person was evident to all
who gathered.[1] This is what happens when
we come to the Word. The water of the Word

> As Ezra gave
> the Word by the
> Water Gate, the
> imagery of water
> pouring forth
> was evident to
> all who gathered.

both nourishes and cleanses our souls. To do this daily, we need two
things: a consistent time and place.

A Consistent Time

"Yes, I'm awake. I'm not up, but I'm awake."

I mumble these words as my husband gets ready for work. Jeff is
one of those cheery types in the morning. Instantly awake. Suffice
it to say, morning is not my best time of day.

Jeff says I'm like an old television set, where a dot of light begins
in the middle of the screen and slowly widens to the outer edges.
That's how I wake up. Slowly. Yes, my Romeo likens me to an old
television set. Endearing, I know.

It is true, though. Mornings are a challenge for me. I'm slug-
gish. Inarticulate. And sometimes less than pleasant. But at night?
I'm wide awake. Focused. Energized. And much more productive.

When I taught English full-time in a public school, my life
revolved around the bell. Sleeping in wasn't an option because arriv-
ing late to work wasn't an option. I had students (not to mention

parents and a principal) who expected me to be in my classroom every morning when they showed up. Somehow this night owl was never late to work.

Having a consistent quiet time in the morning was easy back then. I kept my Bible on my desk (yes, in a public school), and I read it every morning before the first period started. Then I had another baby and again became a stay-at-home mom. A school bell no longer dictated when it was time to start the next class or eat lunch. Instead, I had a crying baby who didn't always follow the same clock I did.

During these blurry years, I tried different strategies for having a quiet time. By "quiet time," I mean a period of time set aside each day to read the Bible and listen to God's voice. Sometimes I woke up extra early. But let's be real. When you've been up every 2.5 hours to nurse a baby, the last thing you want to do is sacrifice more sleep, even to read your Bible. You're barely functional as it is. Or maybe that was just me.

I was pretty sure God understood this, so I used the baby's mid-morning nap to rub my eyes and read my Bible. My best time of day, however, was still at night—especially after the kids were in bed.

Yeah, I know all the verses that show Jesus rising early to find a quiet place alone to pray, and I've heard plenty of "talks" about how we're supposed to have our quiet time in the morning. (I'm convinced only morning people give those talks.) It sounded too legalistic to me. God wants us to spend time with Him every day because we need the water of the Word to nourish and cleanse our souls daily. Does it really matter if I do that at 9:00 p.m. instead of 7:00 a.m.?

The more I wrestled with this issue, the more I kept hearing about firstfruits. In a sermon on Sunday morning. With a friend over a pot of tea. Even in my own Bible reading (at night, thank you).

When a certain word keeps cropping up with unusual consistency, I pay attention. So I did a little word study on firstfruits, and I learned it's all over the Bible. I mean, it's everywhere. From the Old Testament to the New Testament.

Firstfruits were associated with offerings. God wanted the firstfruits because He wanted to be first in people's lives. It goes back to the first commandment He gave to Moses, "You shall have no other gods before Me."[2] Giving God the firstfruits—of time and resources—was the way people demonstrated He was their first priority.

When the exiles returned from Babylon, they were out of practice with the idea of taking an offering to the temple. That wasn't a part of their lives back in Babylon, so Ezra and his contemporary, Nehemiah, had to teach them.

> We will bring the firstfruits of our land...to the LORD's house year by year (Nehemiah 10:35).

They talked about firstfruits at other times too. It was a big deal, so I asked God what it would look like for me to give Him the "firstfruits" in my life. I'm not a farmer, so I can't bring Him the firstfruits of my land. That would yield only a few weeds in a yard that's hard to keep green. How am I to give God the firstfruits of my life today?

> My whole day goes better when I give God the firstfruits of my day.

> Seek first the kingdom of God and His righteousness (Matthew 6:33).

Time. I sensed God telling me, through His Word, that I needed to give Him the firstfruits of my day. To seek Him first. So I tried it. I decided to read one psalm each morning before I did anything else. Most psalms take two or three minutes to read. That's it. Totally doable. Then later in the day, when I felt more awake, or late at night when I felt really awake, I'd dive into whatever book of the Bible I was studying at the time.

Then something unexpected happened. After reading one psalm, I wanted to read more. My morning time, which was a mere nod of obedience at first, grew. It did something else too. Reading God's Word in the morning oriented my thoughts around Him, first and foremost, before beginning my day. Now I can hardly start my day any other way.

I'll never be the bright-eyed morning glory some folks are, yet I've discovered my whole day goes better when I give God the first-fruits of my day. But please hear me...If you're in a season of life when mornings just don't work for you, do not allow shame or guilt to enter into your heart and mind. Find a time that works for you and stick with that. The real key is consistency. God isn't confined to speaking only in the mornings. He's bigger than any rigid schedule we might come up with. But do find a time. That's the most important thing.

A Consistent Place

To be consistent with a daily quiet time, it helps not only to have a designated time of day for *when* you plan to meet with God but also a designated area, most likely in your home, for *where* you plan to meet with Him. Make this your own personal oasis—a place where you can go for spiritual refreshment. Keep your Bible there, along with a pen and journal too.

Not too long ago I spent the better part of a day in my car running errands. They were all important errands, or at least they seemed important at the time. One errand after another ate up my day until none of what I really wanted to do got done. By the time

I got home I was worn-out and a little cranky. Okay, maybe a lot cranky.

I grumbled my way through the kitchen, irritated that I hadn't been able to clean it earlier, and, of course, no one else bothered to clean it either. I complained about the backpacks piled up by the door because I had tripped over one of them—again. And I shuffled around the living room, unhappy with the loads of laundry that seemed to grow on the couch out of nowhere.

My negative thoughts were spiraling downward with negative actions to match. I was out of sorts and struggling to snap out of it. If ever I needed some transformation it was on this icky day when everything irked me. I needed a do-over. Some quiet time away. My heart and mind desperately needed a reset button.

> Time alone in His presence does more to quiet my soul than anything this world can offer.

A reset button for me looks like a few minutes in my quiet chair in the corner of my bedroom. I call it my quiet chair because it's the place I go when I need a respite from my day. It's my oasis.

My quiet chair wasn't expensive, but it reclines just so, with a separate footstool for my feet. There's nothing special about the chair, except it's where my Father meets me. I know He's with me everywhere I go, but my quiet chair is where I go when I need a heart-to-heart with my Father. Time alone in His presence does more to quiet my soul than anything this world can offer. Not coincidentally, my quiet chair is where I read my Bible and then pour out my heart in prayer through the words I write in journals.

On that icky, frustrating day, I made my way to my quiet chair and asked God to show me how I'd gotten so far off-track. With ink on paper, I told Him how sorry I was for my bad attitude, and I asked Him to help me replace my negative thoughts with His truth. I retraced my thought patterns for the day and realized it all started with one small frustration: an unforeseen delay. Which wasn't a big deal. But my frustration was compounded with another unexpected turn. Then another. With each new delay, I entertained more negative thoughts. Soon the train of negativity was barreling through my mind until it led to a train wreck of a mom.

Whenever I have a yucky day like this, what bothers me the most is the fact that I know these frustrations are minor inconveniences, not life-threatening illnesses or life-altering accidents. Believe me, I know! All I have to do is think about what five minutes of everyday life in a wheelchair is like for my brother and I'm undone. So on top of the normal, everyday frustrations is an added layer of guilt for being bothered by them in the first place.

> God's Word is truth and the truth sets us free.

The good news is transformation is possible. When my mind leads me down another trail of negative thinking, I can redirect these thought patterns with the truth of God's Word. Small, negative thoughts may seem harmless in the moment, but if left unchecked, those same negative thoughts grow into negative actions. Thankfully, Paul confirms in his letter to the Romans that renewing our minds is, indeed, possible.

> Do not be conformed to this age, but be transformed by the renewing of your mind, so that you may discern what is the good, pleasing, and perfect will of God (Romans 12:2).

When we take those negative thoughts captive and examine them under the light of God's truth, they lose their power. Because God's Word is truth and the truth sets us free.[3]

Time with God in His Word brings a renewed strength—a quiet confidence—because this is where I'm reminded best that everything's not dependent on me. I forget that sometimes. I start carrying on with my day, and before I know it I'm fretting over small stuff. But God has everything in His hands, and sometimes I need to take a time-out to remind myself He's got everything under control.

If we want to hear the voice of God, we need look no further than His Word. And if the intake of the Word is as important to our spiritual lives as the intake of water is to our physical lives, then we need to read it every day. Yet as soon as we hear a pastor or church leader tell us that, we nod in agreement while mentally running through a list of all the reasons why we can't. In chapter 4 we discussed several of the challenges we face when reading the Bible, but that's to say nothing of the fact that we're just plain busy. It's hard to find the time. Or more accurately, it's hard to *make* the time.

I get it. I do. Even though God didn't create the world to spin any faster than it already does, we spin ourselves faster and faster in the hopes of getting more done. Our culture has accepted a breakneck pace of life as if it's normal. But when we return to the creation story in Genesis 1, we find two essential elements in place before God fills the earth with life.

> God said, "Let there be a space between the waters, to separate the waters of the heavens from the waters of the earth" (1:6 NLT).

Space. Let there be a space. Then God called the space "sky." Notice the order of creation:

- Day 1: Light
- Day 2: Space (Sky)
- Day 3: Dry Ground (Land)
- Day 4: Sun, Moon, Stars
- Day 5: Birds and Fish
- Day 6: Animals and Man

Before God created life on Day 5, He created space on Day 2. Space. Then life.

> Like an empty womb, God will fill the empty space in our lives with new life.

As soon as I have a little space on my calendar, I tend to fill it up quickly. But on the very first page of Scripture, God's Word breathes a fresh message that resonates deep inside my busy little heart: *Create space. Make room for new life.* Like an empty womb, God will fill the empty space in our lives with new life.

Water and space were necessary precursors to life. The same is true for us spiritually. This calls for us to be obedient and patient, though. We need to resist the temptation to fill up the "available time slots" in our schedules. We need to set aside time each day to hear from God. The Word is there, waiting for us to create the space necessary for us to slow down, open its pages, and take it in. When we create space in our hurried schedules to spend time with our Creator, He promises to fill that space with new life as He transforms us from the inside out.

It helps if you have a comfy chair too.

6

The Way We Wait

The Lamb who is at the center of the throne will shepherd
them; He will guide them to springs of living waters, and
God will wipe away every tear from their eyes.

REVELATION 7:17

While wandering hospital hallways, I can't help but devise my own ranking of misery. The Burn Unit is by far the worst. Then the Intensive Care Unit. After that, the Neuro Unit. There are other floors, too, ones that contain milder maladies, but the only cheerful place I can find is the Labor and Delivery Unit. Every once in a while death steals the joy that normally accompanies the birthing rooms. For the most part, though, it's the only floor in the hospital where people smile.

Sometimes I loll about the happy wing, watching old friends and new grandparents bring balloons and presents. But I can take only so much. I resent their bliss while my brother suffers on another floor.

My private jaunts invariably lead me back to the Burn Unit. Hiding in shadows, I listen to the living mummies moan indiscernible utterances of anguish. Their muted cries give voice to what I feel but

> The ones who bring the most comfort come, knowing they can't help, but they can be close.

don't know how to express. So I sit in silence with the mummies. I feel strangely at home here. Among the suffering.

The doctors and nurses...I rarely see their faces, just their rubber-soled feet, walking briskly in and out of rooms, up and down the halls. Always busy about the business of healing. But the people who bring the most healing and comfort—for the wounds so deep I'm afraid they're beyond reach—are the ones, the few, who still come to sit with my mom in the waiting room. They come knowing they can't help, but they can be close.

The waiting room becomes the metaphor for all of life. We're waiting. Waiting for healing to come. For new life to begin.

The more I read the Bible, the more I notice the theme of waiting. In the Old Testament, people are waiting for Christ to come and deliver them. In the New Testament, they're waiting for Christ to return and establish His reign once and for all. I find myself waiting too. I'm waiting for the day when all suffering will end.

> The waiting room becomes the metaphor for all of life. We're waiting. Waiting for healing to come. For new life to begin.

Part of me wants Jesus to return today. I'm ready for the sorrow of this world to be over, but then I read in 2 Peter 3:9: "The Lord does not delay His promise, as some understand delay, but is patient with you, not wanting any to perish but all to come to repentance." Isn't that just like God? He waits and waits because He wants everyone to come to a saving knowledge of Him. This portion of Scripture convicts me because part of me wants to end this time in history and get on with eternity, but the other part of me yearns for everyone to meet Jesus and grow deeper in their relationship with Him.

This is my heart's desire—to equip others to know God and hear His voice through His Word. The challenges of reading the Bible are real but not insurmountable.

At Grandma's house a card table was always set up in the corner of her living room with a puzzle in progress. Next to the scattered pieces, my grandma liked to prop up the cover of the puzzle box. The picture on the front of the box acted as a guide while she sorted the pieces by color, so the blue puzzle pieces were likely for the sky, the green pieces the leaves of the trees, and so forth. I loved it when Grandma let me pick a color group and work on a segment of her puzzle.

I've heard that some people enjoy working puzzles without ever seeing the cover of the box. To me that sounds like a strange form of self-torture. It would take so much longer that way! The cover of the puzzle box provides the complete picture. It helps us see how all the little pieces will eventually come together.

In the same way, when we read the Bible, we come across a lot of different stories. Each story is a piece of a larger picture—a larger story. So it helps to know what that larger picture is.

The Telescope Approach

To garner the big picture of the Bible, we need to read it in its entirety in a reasonably short period of time—usually within a few months to one year. I call this the Telescope Approach. The two primary ways to study the Bible with the Telescope Approach are to

> A reading plan is simply a tool to help you stay on track when your daily reading has become hit and miss.

(1) read the Bible "cover to cover" and (2) read the Bible in chronological order. This gives us the breadth we need for a fuller understanding of the Bible.

The first Telescope Approach is to read from Genesis to Revelation. In the back of this book you'll find a 365-Day Bible Reading Plan that takes you through the Bible, book by book. You can read the whole Bible in a year if you read three, and sometimes four, chapters a day. But don't ever feel pressured to follow a plan dogmatically. A reading plan is simply a tool to help you stay on track when your daily reading has become hit and miss. You can always move through any reading plan at your own pace.

The second Telescope Approach is to read the Bible in chronological order. I've found tremendous benefit in reading the Bible chronologically. Most chronological Bibles have 365 daily readings as well, but they're arranged in the order in which historical events actually occurred.

Both Telescope Approaches provide the bigger picture of God's overarching plan for redemption by covering the seven major eras in history.

ERA ONE—Predestination (Before the Creation of the Universe)

Before the installment of time, God existed. He has no beginning and no end. In Genesis 1:26, it says, "Let Us make man in Our image." Who is "us"? The triune existence of God in three persons—the Father, the Son, the Spirit. In Ephesians 1:4-5, Paul says, "He chose us in Him, before the foundation of the world, to be holy and blameless in His sight. In love He predestined us to be adopted through Jesus Christ for Himself, according to His favor and will." Before God ever said, "Let there be light," He had a plan, and that plan included you and me.[1]

ERA TWO—Creation (Genesis 1–2)

The world we live in, however, did have a starting point. "In the beginning God created the heavens and the earth" (Genesis 1:1). God created shape and order out of a formless void by speaking the world into existence. Then He created the first man and woman, and they enjoyed God's presence in the garden of Eden.

> God doesn't do anything by accident. He's a God of order and design.

ERA THREE—Separation (Genesis 3)

God doesn't do anything by accident. He's a God of order and design. So why did He place the one tree Adam and Even shouldn't eat from right in the middle of the garden?[2] If Adam and Eve were supposed to refrain from eating the fruit on this one tree in question, why didn't God place it in the far corner of the garden? You know, a good day's hike from the general hangout areas in Eden. Was God trying to tempt them with the forbidden fruit every day? No. It's not in God's nature to do so.

When God *planted* the tree there, He was giving Adam and Eve free will. They had a choice, every day, whether they would obey God or not. Every time they walked past that one tree they had to choose: God or self? They eventually chose self and sin entered the world, separating sinful people from a holy God.

ERA FOUR—Expectation (Genesis 4–Malachi)

After Adam and Eve disobeyed God and were expelled from His presence in the garden, we're given a glimpse of God's redemptive plan already in motion. If we look closely at the story of Adam and Eve's first two sons, Cain and Abel, the hope of Jesus is there in Genesis 4.

Abel worked as a shepherd, Cain as a farmer. When the time came to offer a sacrifice, Abel brought "the best of the firstborn lambs" and Cain "presented some of his crops."[3] Cain knew what to bring as an acceptable sacrifice. This is a story of disobedience, not ignorance. He refused to obey, and after his offering was rejected by God, Cain killed his brother out of envy.

In this ancient narrative we hear Scripture whisper the foretelling of Christ. Look at the similarities:

Abel	Jesus
A shepherd	The Good Shepherd
Shedding the blood of a lamb	Shedding His own blood as the Lamb of God
Murdered out of rebellious envy	Crucified out of rebellious envy
Betrayed by his own brother	Betrayed by His own Hebrew brethren

The story of Cain and Abel is more than a story of brotherhood gone awry. It illustrates a real expectation because it foreshadows the coming of Christ, who would make a way for God's people to be in His presence once again. So when we read the Old Testament, from Genesis 4 all the way through Malachi, we want to read with expectant eyes on Christ. We don't have to wait until the New Testament to find Jesus, because He's already there in the narratives of old.

> When we read the Old Testament, we want to read with expectant eyes on Christ.

ERA FIVE—*Salvation (Matthew–John)*

The entire Old Testament reads like a drumroll, stirring our hearts in expectation, explaining how we'll recognize Christ when He comes. This is why the first chapter of Matthew opens with a genealogy. It's a quick recap of Genesis to Malachi, and it leads us straight to Jesus.

The four Gospel accounts give us four distinct but unifying vantage points on the life, death, and resurrection of Jesus. Together they render a more complete picture, and that picture culminates in a torn veil in the temple where the ark of the covenant resided, providing access to the very presence of God.

> The veil of the temple was torn in two from top to bottom (Matthew 27:51 NKJV).

Torn from top to bottom. This little detail tells a lot. Access to God's holy presence didn't come about from bottom to top; it didn't come about from us reaching up to God through any good work of our own. Access to God's holy presence came about from top to bottom, from God coming to earth, becoming one of us and giving Himself for us so He could redeem us and restore us to a right relationship with Him.

Access to God's presence through Christ's redemptive work on the cross is available to all who believe and surrender their lives to Him.

> If we confess our sins, He is faithful and righteous to forgive us our sins and to cleanse us from all unrighteousness (1 John 1:9).

God cleanses us on the inside. We're redeemed by His grace. Now we embark on the journey of transformation, of growing to become more like Jesus, and a new waiting begins.

ERA SIX—*Transformation (Acts–Jude)*

Like the period of *expectation* in the Old Testament, the period of *transformation* is a second kind of waiting. This time we wait for Jesus to return in glory, but our waiting is not an idle one. We have kingdom work to do. When God placed Adam and Eve in the garden of Eden, He assigned tasks for them to tend the garden. When the Hebrew exiles returned to Jerusalem, each person had a job to fulfill, a part to play in rebuilding the temple, the city, and the city walls.

> We're here to bring God glory, and we do that by becoming more like Him.

We have a job to do as well. Once we've surrendered our lives to Jesus, we become new people, and the divine purpose God has intended for us since before the beginning of time becomes our kingdom work.

My college students often ask, "What should I do in life?" The answer is easy: We're here to bring God glory, and we do that by becoming more like Him. With each passing day we're to grow in His likeness in ever-increasing measure. Paul put it like this:

> All of us who have had that veil removed can see and reflect the glory of the Lord. And the Lord—who is the Spirit—makes us more and more like him as we are changed into his glorious image (2 Corinthians 3:18 NLT).

The way we're transformed into Christ's likeness is by being immersed in the life-changing truth of God's Word, reading the Bible regularly. From Acts to Jude, we're given a breadth of stories and instructions to help us in the waiting, to help us be transformed.

ERA SEVEN—Consummation (Revelation)

One of the greatest metaphors in the Bible depicts Christ as the Bridegroom and the church as His bride. The act of redemption was an act of betrothal, and the engagement is permanent. A wedding is going to take place, and it won't be called off.

The book of Revelation is apocalyptic in nature, yet it describes a great wedding banquet that will one day take place. When Jesus returns, He won't come as a baby in a manger. Not this time. In the second coming of Christ we'll see the King of all kings, and there will be a tremendous celebration and feast.

> Then I heard something like the voice of a vast multitude, like the sound of cascading waters, and like the rumbling of loud thunder, saying: "Hallelujah, because our Lord God, the Almighty, has begun to reign! Let us be glad, rejoice, and give Him glory, because the marriage of the Lamb has come, and His [bride] has prepared herself" (Revelation 19:6-7).

The seven major eras in history—predestination, creation, separation, expectation, salvation, transformation, and consummation—help us piece together the individual stories in the Bible to form a more complete picture of the biblical story as a whole. It's popular to describe a Bible study as "deep" to assure someone of its merit. This usually means going deep into one small passage, poring over a few verses while seeking their original meaning in the Hebrew or Greek.

> The beauty of Scripture is found in the way it tells one grand story in so many different ways.

But if that's the only way we ever study the Bible, we'll miss the larger picture. For a deeper study of the Bible, we need both depth and breadth. The Telescope Approach gives us the breadth we need.

The beauty of Scripture is found in the way it tells this one grand story in so many different ways. When David became king and learned his friend Jonathan had died in battle, he conducted a search throughout the country for Jonathan's remaining relatives. He discovered Jonathan had one living son, Mephibosheth, who had injured his feet in a terrible fall as a young boy and was unable to walk. King David invited Mephibosheth to dine at the king's table every day for the rest of his life.

This story in the Old Testament foreshadows the coming King in Revelation. We've all been broken by the Fall. We've all been sought by the King. And we've all been invited to His table for eternity. But until eternity arrives, we're here on this earth—waiting. We may not have broken feet, but we have broken souls. We were born into a lost and broken world, and somewhere along life's path we stumbled and fell.

My brother's feet were physically disabled in a terrible accident at a young age, but the truth is, we're all limping our way through life in one way or another, waiting for the great Healer to come and restore our brokenness, to make us whole.

In the meantime, we've got work to do.

7

The Time We Spend

This Book of the Law shall not depart from your mouth, but you shall meditate on it day and night, so that you may be careful to do according to all that is written in it.

JOSHUA 1:8 ESV

Long before a car accident changed the trajectory of our lives, my brother and I would walk to a creek behind our house and he'd teach me how to fish. Kendall had a tackle box. Inside each little compartment lay a hook or weight or bobber. Admittedly, I was more fascinated with the tackle box than anything happening beneath the water's surface. The tiny hooks shimmered in bright hues of turquoise and orange, and I learned there's a bait for every kind of fish.

Some say fishing is more art than science while others insist it's more science than art. It's definitely a bit of both. A process is involved. Like how to find your spot near the water. How to thread a line. How to choose your hook and weight. But then? Fishing requires patience. You never know when a fish might bite.

On Wednesday morning the women at my church gather around tables with their Bibles and colored pens. A few bring a

Greek lexicon and a Bible dictionary with them. Each person's Bible "bag" is like a tackle box with our own little hooks to catch some truth or reel in some hope. We love our Wednesday mornings together, diving into the Word. Reading. Sharing. Laughing. Praying. And sometimes crying.

One morning a visitor named Kathryn joined us. She was new to church and new to Bible study, and she shared a powerful story of how she had recently met the living God. For the first time in her life she believed He was real. So she thought she should go to church. But she was a little nervous.

Kathryn surveyed our colored pens and notebooks, her eyes wide with apprehension.

> God's Word isn't just for scholars in seminaries— it's for everyone.

When one friend shared a few synonyms from her Greek lexicon, Kathryn tossed her head back and laughed, saying, "Well, it's all Greek to me!"

We all laughed because we could all relate.

As the weeks passed, Kathryn and I shared our stories and got to know each other. I watched her faith deepen as her familiarity with the Bible grew. She confessed to me privately, though, that some parts of the Bible intimidated her, and she still wasn't sure what to do with all those colored pens. Right then and there I wanted to create a Bible study for women. A study for the brand-new believer as well as the seasoned veteran of the faith. Because God's Word isn't just for Bible scholars in seminaries—it's for everyone.

Meeting Kathryn reminded me of the first time I read the Bible. Indeed, certain passages seemed to come alive while other passages confused me. So I'll share with you what I shared with my friend Kathryn. We don't need a huge tackle box to tackle the Bible.

Getting Started

All you really need to get started is a Bible and a pen. I mentioned earlier that I found a study Bible helpful as a new reader of the Bible. As a teen I viewed the commentary on the bottom half of the page like CliffsNotes, a shortcut for learning. I quickly discovered, however, that the introductions to each book of the Bible proved most helpful. The introductions help us glean the necessary background information by answering these questions:

- Who wrote the book?
- To whom was the book written?
- When was the book written?
- What was the author's main purpose for writing the book?

Once you have a general understanding of a book's background, I encourage you to dive in and discover for yourself what the book says.

> We don't need a huge tackle box to tackle the Bible.

When I began studying the Bible, I didn't have a formula or any tools at my disposal. I didn't know there were any, but with my study Bible and a pen, I developed a simple three-step pattern: Read it. Write it. Pray it.

Read It

Before I read my Bible, I pray this simple prayer from Psalm 119:18:

> Open my eyes that I may see wonderful things in your law (NIV).

Reading seems straightforward enough, but to comprehend the biblical text with greater accuracy, we want to read each book of the Bible all the way through, from beginning to end. With our first reading, the goal is to grasp the overall gist of the book. Then we can read the text again, but this time slower, focusing on each passage to consider, first, what it says about God's character. God has revealed Himself in His Word, and our primary focus when studying the Bible is to know Him better. Next, we want to notice which passages do the following:

- Declare a truth.
- Give a command.
- Post a warning.
- Present a promise.
- Share a prayer.
- Offer an example.

Not every verse falls neatly into one of these categories, so write down any questions you have about the text. Some of your questions will be answered right away with further reading while other questions might take longer. Be willing to wait for the answers. Remember the wise men? They spent two years journeying toward Jesus after He was born. We won't need that long to understand the major parts of the Bible, but we do need to be committed for the long haul, trusting that a fuller understanding of the Bible will indeed come with time.

Then try reading the book again in another version. Reading the same book of the Bible in a few different versions helps to render a fuller understanding of the intended meaning. This is where apps come in handy. You can always read a different version with a free app to supplement your reading.

A cornerstone of solid Bible study is to allow Scripture to interpret Scripture.[1] In other words, students of the Bible are wise to interpret a specific passage in light of what the rest of the Bible has to say about that topic. We never want to read a passage in isolation. We want to take in the surrounding text while also considering the other passages in the Bible that speak to the same topic. Part

> Writing the Word helps us slow down and prevents us from skimming too quickly over the text.

of the beauty of God's Word is the remarkable consistency in its message. When we look to Scripture for the interpretation of Scripture, we're taking in the whole counsel of God's Word.

Write It

I always keep a journal next to my Bible. Any inexpensive notebook will do. A key way to immerse ourselves in the life-changing truth of God's Word is to write it out, word for word. Yep, just write it. Writing the Word helps us slow down and prevents us from skimming too quickly over the text. It's the most straightforward way we can saturate our hearts and minds with the truth of God's Word. I'll discuss writing the Word in greater depth in the next chapter, but for now, rest assured in the sweet simplicity of this step. It's what the scribes did for centuries. Like Ezra, they wrote the Word.

Plenty of study methods are available to us—taking notes, outlining an entire book of the Bible, paraphrasing the biblical text in our own words, or committing Bible verses to memory. All of these methods are valid, but writing the Word is a beautifully simple endeavor that yields abundant fruit in our lives. Because God's Word never returns void.[2]

Pray It

How should we respond to Scripture? The same way we started. Just as we begin our daily quiet time in prayer (by praying the words of Psalm 119:18), we finish our quiet time in prayer. We give God our gratitude for who He is and ask Him to reveal how we might apply what we've just read. Is there a statement of truth we're struggling to believe? A warning we need to heed? A command we need to follow? Or a prayer we need to make our own? We can respond to God's Word by talking to Him about the passage we just read and asking Him to help us put His Word into action.

> The Telescope Approach gives us the breadth we need and the Microscope Approach gives us the depth we need.

In chapter 6 I wrote about the importance of the Telescope Approach—gleaning the bigger picture of God's redemption of humanity by reading the Bible "cover to cover" or chronologically. Even with the Telescope Approach, we can still follow these three simple steps: Read it. Write it. Pray it. When I'm reading three or four chapters in one sitting, I may not write all of it down, but I do write down the one or two verses that most resonated with me.

The Microscope Approach

The Telescope Approach gives us the breadth we need and the Microscope Approach gives us the depth we need. For greater depth, there are four basic kinds of Bible studies: character studies, topical studies, word studies, and book studies.

In a character study, we examine the life of a person in the Bible. We get to know God better by seeing how He interacts with His people.

In a topical study, we search the Scriptures to learn what the Bible teaches about a specific subject. With cross-references and a concordance we can find other verses that deal with the same topic.

In a word study, we explore the Scriptures with the aid of other reference tools to understand the fuller use and meaning of a word in the original Hebrew or Greek.

In a book study, we learn the individual books of the Bible by discovering the historical context, literary form, and authorial intent.

I've enjoyed all four kinds, but I prefer book studies most of the time. When we study an individual book of the Bible, we gain a deeper appreciation for that author's contribution to the overarching story of redemption. Book studies also provide the necessary context for the characters, topics, and words we find within them. Context is key.

A small package arrived in the mail for me—a birthday gift from my mom. When I opened it, my oldest daughter looked inside the box and said, "I don't get it."

I did.

Mom had sent me her Bible. Her old one.

The small red leather Bible I saw her carry to church when I was little.

> The greatest gift we can ever give our children is a heritage of the Word.

The same Bible I saw her read countless times. The same Bible she clutched when sitting by her son's hospital bed.

Mom's small red Bible is worn around the edges and marked on the pages—evidence of much use. She's been using a different Bible for some time now, but this is the Bible I remember from when I was growing up.

The greatest gift we can ever give our children is a heritage of the Word.

My mom's Bible can be held in one hand. It's nothing like the massive relic stationed in the hospital chapel; that Bible seemed more ornamental than transformational. It wasn't the kind of Bible you could write notes or questions or prayers in its margins.

I've seen other Bibles that looked almost as unused as that one. But that's not what our Bibles are for. They're not for decorating coffee tables or sitting on shelves with special editions of classic literature. Bibles are for reading, learning, growing, praying, and changing. Bibles are for consuming.

> A broken binding binds the broken.

Before the advent of laptops and e-books, a teacher had two kinds of books in the classroom—textbooks and workbooks. Everybody knows you don't write in a textbook. Those books need to last for years, but workbooks are consumable. Students are *supposed* to write on the pages. They can write their names on the front, and they can write on every single page inside. At the end of the school-year it's theirs. They can keep it.

Someone along the way figured out that students learn best when they're actively engaged in the process—putting pen to paper, thoughts into words. I see my Bible the same way. It's more like a workbook than a textbook. The Bible invites me into its pages. To wrestle with its contents. To ask questions in its margins. To write verses in its open spaces. After circling, highlighting, and underlining the words and phrases that grab my attention, the binding on my Bible inevitably loosens. But that's okay. I'm convinced a broken binding binds the broken. Because I've seen it in my life.

Destructive thought patterns have been rerouted to think on things that are pure and lovely and noble and true. When I'm actively reading and writing the words in my Bible, my natural inclination to justify my actions is met with truth. This is why James likens the Word of God to a mirror.[3] A mirror reflects the outer person while the Bible reflects the inner person. When I'm peering into the mirror of God's Word, the darkness in my heart is revealed with the light of His truth. I can't ignore or justify or rationalize my poor choices anymore. The truth won't let me.

The only "clean and pristine" Bible I own is my newest one. When I read through an individual book, I use a red pen the first time for writing my thoughts and questions on the page. With a second reading, I use a green pen. With a third, purple. A fourth, orange. The colors on the page reveal the progression of my thoughts. Sometimes I'll see a purple-ink answer to a red-ink question. This tells me it took three readings before I really grasped something, which also affirms that deeper understanding does come with practice and patience. The more I work in my Book, the more my Book works in me. God gave us His Word so we'll consume it.

> The more I work in my Book, the more my Book works in me.

Every Bible I own represents a season in my life. My pink faux leather NIV study Bible is the Bible I used in my late teens and early twenties. When I got married I bought a navy-blue Bible so I could have my married name printed on the front. In my early thirties I needed another new one. This time I went with black. I'm currently using an ESV study Bible and loving it.

Someday I plan to give my Bibles to my kids the same way my mom gave her old red Bible to me. They won't be pretty gifts. They'll be worn and used. But my kids will see my notes and my questions and my thought processes. More than anything they'll see the most important part of my life. Those Bibles with broken bindings and worn edges and scribbled-on pages are the evidence of a life that desperately seeks to know God in deeper ways and hear His voice. I know I'd be lost without Him, and I believe with all my heart that His voice is the voice that matters most.

One of the first Bible verses I committed to memory was 1 Peter 5:7: "Cast all your anxiety on him because he cares for you" (NIV). I liked this verse because it says Jesus wants to carry my burdens. I can go to Him with everything.

When I wrote this verse in my notebook, I stopped after the first word: *cast*. I don't know why I never saw it before, but when Peter penned the inspired words we find in 1 Peter 5:7, he used imagery familiar to his trade. Peter was a fisherman and a fisherman *casts* a net.

Whenever I picture a net in my mind, I think of the kind my brother brought with us to the creek. If we (I should say *he*) caught a fish, he took that net and scooped up the fish. But that's not the kind of net Peter used with his fishing partners James and John. Their nets were more than 15 feet in diameter, tied with thick ropes, and heavy enough to require two men, one on each side, to heave them into the water. Casting a fisherman's net meant exerting a lot of physical strength.

Peter was a fisherman-turned-follower-of-Christ, but he also had a wife, extended family, and a home. Surely he experienced the same tug and pull of responsibilities we experience today. Our to-do lists can be exhausting. Situations beyond our control can feel overwhelming. Worry, fear, and doubt are the natural companions of anxiety.

Yet we are called to *cast* our anxiety onto Jesus, for He cares for us and He's strong enough to take on our heaviest burdens. Peter knows it's not easy to leave our concerns and worries at the feet of Jesus. He knows it might take all the strength we have, or whatever strength we have left, to lay our burdens at the cross.

Whenever I'm tempted to cling to a burden, I think of the word *cast* and remember the picture Peter paints in Scripture. I'm not sure I would have made the connection if I hadn't written the verse on paper, word for word, noticing each word and the meaning each one carries.

> The ones who wrote the Word most, knew the Word best.

The importance of reading the Word, writing it, and praying it can't be emphasized enough. In biblical times those who knew the Scriptures best were the scribes. Ezra's life as a scribe is evidence of this fact. His love for God's Word permeated every facet of his life, and he trained others to take on the discipline of copying Scripture by hand, and the tradition continued long after Ezra's last breath. The scribes who copied Scripture, word for word, were the ones who taught Scripture to others. The ones who wrote the Word most, knew the Word best.

The same can be said of us today. When we write Scripture by hand, we learn it and retain it in ways that can't be rivaled by other methods. A pen and paper are still today the best hook and bait we can have in our "tackle box" for the Bible.

8

The Words We Write

Go now, write it on a tablet for them, inscribe it on a scroll,
that for the days to come it may be an everlasting witness.

ISAIAH 30:8 NIV

My small group from church gathers in a friend's living room to read through the Gospel of John. One person reads a chapter aloud and then pauses, giving everyone a chance to ask questions. We discuss that chapter and then move on to the next one. At one point a friend asks, "How can you tell when God is speaking to you? I mean, how do you really know it's God's voice you're hearing and not your own random thoughts?"

It's a fair question. We want to be sure we're not making decisions based on a whim. We want to *know* when it's really God speaking and not last night's egg salad sandwich. But how?

I go back to July 31, 1990, alone on a mountaintop. I'd been attending church my whole life. I had sensed God's presence during worship. I had prayed "the prayer" as a kid, sincerely asking Jesus to come into my heart. I'd been baptized shortly thereafter in a river. But it wasn't until that day at camp, while reading the Bible, that I heard God's voice. Not audibly, but distinctly. Something so wholly other that

> The voice of God never contradicts what is written in His Word.

I knew it couldn't be my own thoughts because my thoughts were bent on self-destruction and had been for years. God's voice spoke *life*.

The more I read God's Word the more I hear God saying I'm His beloved. He knit me together in my mother's womb, He has started something good in me, He promises to complete it, and He wants me to give of myself and serve others.

Nowhere in the Bible does it say it would be better for me to just end it all right now. Nowhere in the Bible does it say everyone would be better off if I weren't around. Nowhere in the Bible does it say I should do whatever I want and it won't matter. Nowhere! The voice of God is light and life. The difference is unmistakable.

> By His Word we will know His voice.

So when my friend asks how we can really know if it's God speaking, part of me wants to jump out of my chair and cry, "How can you *not* know?" When we read God's Word, we hear His voice right there on the pages. Over and over He speaks with consistency. The voice of God never contradicts what is written in His Word. He will never tell us to fulfill our own selfish desires. God tells us to put other people's interests ahead of our own. He even goes so far as to tell us to pray for our enemies. Not only that, but He says if our enemies are hungry, we should feed them, and if our enemies are thirsty, we should give them something to drink.

God's voice is so contrary to what we hear every day in this world the difference is radical. The world tells us to satisfy our needs and our cravings with whatever means available. To accumulate more possessions and live in self-indulgence. To promote ourselves and lift ourselves up. But God's path runs counter to our culture. And the only way to know His voice is to hear what He says in His Word. By His Word we will know His voice.

This is why Ezra called for a town meeting by the Water Gate. He knew the only hope they had was to know God through the hearing of His Word. And the citizens of Jerusalem—the exiles who had come out of captivity in Babylon—were so hungry for truth they stood while Ezra read aloud. From daybreak until noon! Can you imagine a church service lasting from sunrise till midday? And they stood the whole time! Do we have that same hunger and desire for truth today?

When I started reading the Bible, I didn't have a Greek lexicon or a fancy set of commentaries, but I enjoyed scribbling words on paper. So I wrote down Bible verses to help commit them to memory. I wrote out whole psalms to meditate on them. I even wrote out the passages I struggled to understand. Writing the Word became a regular part of my daily quiet time, and over time God's Word transformed me from the inside out.

> A Bible study doesn't have to be complicated to be deep.

I'm convinced a Bible study doesn't have to be complicated to be deep. I do love the wonderful tools we have available to us through commentaries and lexicons and the sort, but my favorite time in the Word is when it's just Jesus and me—with a Bible, a journal, and a pen.

Writing the Word helps me internalize what I'm reading. The words of Scripture then seep into my prayers. The more I immerse myself in the truth of God's Word, the more the language of Scripture becomes my language too. I discovered this truth early on: As I write God's truth on paper, He writes His truth on my heart.

In ancient Greece, Plato taught literacy and public speaking skills to his students, but only the wealthy could attend school and learn how to read and write. He lived in an oral culture, and he feared if writing utensils became widespread—where even the "commoners" could learn to read and write—everyone would become forgetful and it would be the end of civilization as they knew it.[1] But that didn't happen. In fact, the opposite did.

> As I write God's truth on paper, He writes His truth on my heart.

Contrary to Plato's fear, writing something down helps us remember better. When we write it, we remember it. As a college professor, I see this in my own classroom. When students take notes, they perform better on tests and quizzes than the students who only listen with their ears. Studies have confirmed the same thing I've observed in my classroom.[2]

Sadly, literacy is increasingly at risk once again. Not because the general population can't afford books and writing utensils as in Plato's day, but because our culture is increasingly dependent on digital media. Screen time has replaced book time. In just 15 years I've witnessed a dramatic shift in literacy among young people in my classroom. Yes, some students take to books like fish to water, but more often than not I see young people struggling to engage with written text. If I give assigned reading in a book, many would rather go home and listen to an audio version than read it for themselves.

On top of this gravitational pull toward all things electronic, the art of handwriting is also rapidly fading in America. The federally adopted standards for education no longer require longhand to be taught in public schools.[3] Students in kindergarten and first grade are taught to print letters, and by second grade they transition to the computer and keyboarding skills.

Writing in longhand, however, has been proven to be more than an eccentric teacher's preference. Studies have shown college students who takes notes with their laptops can, indeed, type faster and record a greater quantity of words than their peers who take notes by hand. But the latter have demonstrated a superior ability for processing the information in their own words and for retaining the information compared to their technologically oriented colleagues. In short, writing in longhand enhances our memory over typing the same information.[4] Without a doubt writing something down helps us learn and retain what we've written.

This is not to say I'm anti-technology. Not at all. I'm grateful for the many conveniences technology offers. But I still recognize the tremendous value that tactile, sensory-stimulating activities provide.

> Writing the Word is a deliberate act to refuse the tyranny of hurry.

With the technology we have at our fingertips, writing by hand might seem old-fashioned and unnecessary, but it has intrinsic benefits scientific research has begun to support. From my own experience, both personally and professionally, I've observed the following ten benefits from writing by hand.

Writing by Hand Helps Us...

1. *Slow our pace.* We've trained our eyes to skim quickly over text, to look for key points and pictures. When we write by hand, we're forcing our eyes to slow down.

2. *Dive deeper into the text.* By slowing our pace we're able to dive deeper into the text supporting those key points, which is usually made up of examples or statistics or quotes, providing more ideas to associate with the key

points, which in turn help us remember the key points
better.

3. *Focus better with fewer distractions.* Our eyes know
how to go through the motion of reading without
comprehending. But when we're writing the text, we
notice when our hands have stopped moving across the
page.

4. *Connect a mental activity with a physical one.* The
learning areas of our brains light up when we tie a
mental exercise to a physical one. Like the kind of
kinetic movement that happens when our fine-motor
skills, such as writing with a pen, coincides with the
mental process of reading.

5. *Process information in more manageable portions.* Reading
is processing. All those strung-together words create
intended meaning, and when we write the words,
we're able to process their meaning in smaller, more
manageable portions.

6. *Become better observers.* Not every key word gets its
own featured text box in the margin. So the ability to
notice the key words within the actual text deepens our
understanding. Writing leads to noticing.

7. *Stitch the parts together.* Many Bibles include subtitles
over the passages, which have been added to the original
biblical text and create artificial breaks. Writing the
Word stitches together the original flow by leaving out
the inserted subtitles.

8. *Internalize the text.* We can read the text with our eyes
and hear it with our ears, but when we write the text

with our hands we're adding another dimension of learning through repetition. Such repetition is crucial for internalizing a text.

9. *Memorize the text.* When we write a passage and then speak it out loud, over and over, we create neural pathways in our brains that reinforce what we're memorizing.

10. *Quiet our hearts and minds.* Something about the discipline of putting pen to paper quiets the soul the way David's harp soothed Saul.[5] Writing the Word is a deliberate act to refuse the tyranny of hurry. It's a way of saying the words of Scripture are worth savoring—each and every one.

Quality time in God's Word can't be reduced to a formula because a relationship isn't fostered by following a checklist of dos and don'ts. A relationship grows when people invest in one another by spending time together, and our relationship with God is no different. We get to know Him when we read and study His Word. Over time I've gathered more resources, kind of like my own tackle box. A Bible dictionary. A Greek and Hebrew lexicon. Study Bibles in other translations. And commentaries too. After studying a book of the Bible myself, I like to hear what others have to say about that book.

> Writing the Word immerses me in Scripture like nothing else can.

These are all great resources to supplement my study time, but I still write out Scripture every day. Sometimes I'll write an entire chapter of a book I'm reading. Sometimes I'll write a few verses that really speak to me regarding something specific in my life. Writing the Word immerses me in Scripture like nothing else can.

When I wrote a Bible study called *Word Writers*, I was asked in an interview to explain my new method. I didn't know how to answer the question because, well, it's not a new method. Writing the Word is as old as the scribes of ancient Jerusalem. *Word Writers* is an invitation to return to the paths of old, to study Scripture the way the scribes studied Scripture—writing the Word by hand. The prophet Jeremiah said:

> This is what the LORD says: "Stand by the roadways and look. Ask about the ancient paths: 'Which is the way to what is good?' Then take it and find rest for yourselves" (6:16).

The ancient paths are the ways that have proven true for thousands of years.

So when my friend at small group wants to know how she can be sure it's really God's voice she's hearing and not just a random thought she's having, my response is the same: We know His voice when we know His Word.

9

The Prayers We Keep

Pray in the Spirit on all occasions with all kinds of
prayers and requests. With this in mind, be alert and
always keep on praying for all the Lord's people.

EPHESIANS 6:18 NIV

After church I walked to the foyer where two ladies sat behind a table, and I signed up for the weekly prayer meeting. The following Thursday morning I gathered with women thrice my age while burping a newborn on my shoulder. The lady in charge passed out a prayer agenda. It started with the president of the United States, the governor of California, and the mayor of our city. Then it listed our pastor and every elder. Next it mentioned several families in the church that had special needs. Someone had done their homework, and I learned some things about several families I felt uncomfortable knowing.

After we prayed for everyone on the list, I scooped up the soft baby toys I used to occupy my infant daughter's attention, but then realized the prayer meeting wasn't over. Apparently the second half was just beginning as the prayer leader looked around the room and asked, "Who has a praise report or a prayer request?"

Each woman around the circle offered a praise report followed by another prayer request, and we prayed right then and there for that specific need. I quickly discerned that making a prayer request wasn't optional. Everyone participated, so when it was my turn, I tried to think of something I needed prayer for, which meant I needed to think of something bad happening in my life for us to pray about. At least that's how all the other prayer requests went, and I didn't want to offer up a frivolous request, like for my daughter to start sleeping through the night.

When it was my turn, I absorbed the silence and the stares as I felt an internal pressure mounting. But I couldn't think of anything bad enough to pray for. So I laid down my cards. I'd recently moved to the area and had attended this church for only a few months. These ladies didn't know a thing about me, so I told them about my brother. That he'd been in a wheelchair for about a decade. And that he could get around pretty well with the use of his arms, but sometimes he got pressure sores and needed to lie in bed, flat on his stomach for several months at a time to allow a pressure sore to heal. He was currently on bedrest with another pressure sore. Could we pray for that?

The women stirred in their seats, visibly moved to prayer, especially for this new need in their midst.

The following week we gathered again and prayed in the same order as the week prior. The president. The governor. The mayor. Then the church leadership and designated families. When it was time to pray for each other, the women shared reports of answered prayer. To this everyone shouted hearty amens and hallelujahs. The women then turned to me and asked if my brother was any better. He wasn't. So the mood shifted to serious again and we prayed some more.

I attended the prayer meeting for several more Thursdays, and each week they asked me if my brother was better. But he wasn't and I sensed a growing concern. Something wasn't working and that something must be me. All the other prayers were promptly answered within a week or two, but not mine.

My presence seemed to dampen the expected amens and hallelujahs, so I stopped going. The prayer meetings, I soon realized, came with an unspoken expectation—that God would answer our prayers the way we wanted Him to, and He would do so in a timely fashion. But that's not the God I'd grown to know and that's not the way I'd learned to pray.

If I learned anything the year I was 12 and wandered hospital hallways, it's that God doesn't always answer our prayers the way we want Him to. God didn't heal my brother. He still endures periodic stretches of hospital stays and imposed bedrests at home. It's maddening. If there's a prayer I could pray to make my brother whole, I'd pray it. I'd do anything. But that's not how prayer works.

> Prayer doesn't give us the thing we want; it gives us the Person we need.

The main problem with prayer is when we confuse requests with demands. Prayer is not a bartering system, where we exchange our words of want for fully satisfied desires.

Prayer doesn't give us the thing we want; it gives us the Person we need.

Prayer is more about communing than receiving. We do receive many blessings through prayer. Those blessings, though, are oftentimes the byproduct of prayer, not the actual purpose of prayer. Prayer is the means by which we commune with God. It's a conversation, and like any good conversation it involves both speaking and listening.

I stepped through the doors of the hotel, eager to check in so I could collapse onto the bed in my room. I had left my house approximately 15 hours earlier and flown overnight, from the West Coast to the East Coast, only to discover in the wee hours of the morning that the second leg of my flight had been canceled. Not delayed. Canceled.

Several hours later, my newly scheduled flight commenced after another long delay on the tarmac. By the time I reached my hotel room, I had spent hours between places, between planes. The delays and detours were almost comical, like some invisible force was thwarting my every effort to arrive at my destination—a conference for Christian women writers where I would speak on the topic of writing. Then the weirdest thing happened. I lost my voice. I felt fine but could barely speak above a whisper.

For the first part of the conference, I spent more time in my room than usual, trying to save my voice for my session. I paced and prayed in my room. *Lord, please strengthen my voice. At least for a few hours?*

When the time came for me to speak, my voice was a little stronger, but not much. About halfway through my talk, I'm pretty sure my voice squeaked like a boy in puberty. Such a bummer. It wasn't at all how I envisioned my presentation going, but the room was packed and the women were gracious. I loved being with them, talking about writing. Still, I was disappointed that I wasn't 100 percent. When I returned to my room, I pulled off my earrings, slipped out of my heels, and removed the lanyard that hung from my neck. I stood there for a moment looking at my name tag. Beneath my name it said *Speaker.* I sighed.

Lord, I came here to speak, but without a voice, I couldn't exactly do that very well. If there's something You want me to learn from this, please show me what it is.

The verse I pray most often tumbled from my lips. *Speak, for Your servant is listening.*[1]

I looked at my name tag again and the word *Speaker*. Then I remembered how my friend Annie had taken a Sharpie, crossed out the word ~~Speaker~~, and written the word *Listener* on her name tag.

Listener.

More words from Scripture came to mind, this time from Psalm 46:10 (NIV):

> *Be still, and know that I am God.*

Be still. And listen. Just listen. *Okay, God, help me to be a good listener.*

I spent the rest of the weekend trying to listen. I rejoined the women at the conference and participated in many wonderful conversations. I couldn't talk much, but I could listen. I found myself asking more and talking less. *Tell me your story. Where are you from? What do you write about?* And I'd listen.

I went to this conference to be a speaker, but I ended up a listener. And something tells me that's just how God wanted it.

When I returned home, the word *listen* continued to beat in my heart. When I read news stories of human turmoil and was tempted to turn the page, the Holy Spirit nudged me to pause, to listen. When I met a new person at church and wanted to move past the awkwardness of not knowing what to say, I sensed a familiar stirring in my soul to wait, to listen. When I talked with God in prayer, longing for His direction, I heard the now-familiar refrain: be still, and listen.

> To be still and listen has become the quiet anthem of my prayer life.

To be still and listen has become the quiet anthem of my prayer life.

For years I thought of Bible study as one activity and prayer as another. You know, read it, write it, and *then* pray it. This is a great starting point, for sure. But the more I read and write Scripture, and the more I practice the discipline of silence, the less I see my time in the Word and my time in prayer as two separate activities. Scripture and prayer have become inextricably intertwined. The one informs the other, and the latter returns me to the former.

> Scripture and prayer have become inextricably intertwined. The one informs the other, and the latter returns me to the former.

I find great value in the Telescope Approach, reading the Bible from beginning to end to garner the overarching story of redemption. But when it comes to prayer, I lean on the Microscope Approach. I select one passage and read it several times. Then I "RAP." Here's what I mean:

The Bible gives us a plethora of prayers to model our own prayers after. (I've included several in the back of this book.) The most famous, of course, is the prayer Jesus taught His disciples, which we call The Lord's Prayer. All the prayers of the Bible include at least one or all of the following three elements: Recognition, Admission, or Petition (RAP). Since we've been talking about the Hebrews' exile in Babylon and their return to Jerusalem, we can look to the great 9-9-9 prayers in the Bible to see the RAP elements of prayer in action.

We find the great 9-9-9 prayers in Daniel 9, Ezra 9, and Nehemiah 9. Daniel was taken captive and lived in Babylon as an exile, and there he prayed the first of these three prayers recorded in Scripture. Ezra led the second caravan of exiles home to Jerusalem and Nehemiah led the third caravan, and in Jerusalem—as the exiles were struggling to restore their way of life—Ezra and Nehemiah each prayed another of the great prayers. Each prayer is almost a chapter long, so I won't include the entire text here. But I'll highlight key portions so you can see how recognition, admission, and petition are included in biblical prayer. Let's look at Daniel's prayer, the one he offered during his bondage in Babylon.

Recognition

When we pray, we want to recognize who God is and what He has done.

> Ah, Lord—the great and awe-inspiring God who keeps
> His gracious covenant with those who love Him and
> keep His commands...(Daniel 9:4).

Daniel begins his prayer by acknowledging the truth about who God is. He's a God who keeps His promises.

Admission

When we pray, we need to admit who we are and what we've done. This takes recognition to another level because we not only recognize who we are and what we've done; we also admit that who we are is so far less than who God is, and what we've done has made us unworthy of being in His presence.

> ...we have sinned, done wrong, acted wickedly, rebelled,
> and turned away from Your commands and ordinances
> (Daniel 9:5).

This is an admission of who we are and what we've done. While Daniel refers specifically to the exiles in Babylon and his ancestors before him, we can all find ourselves in these words. We've all turned away from God's commands at some point in our lives and chosen our own way apart from Him.[2]

Petition

When we pray, we want to petition God's mercy and blessing for ourselves and others.

> Lord, in keeping with all Your righteous acts, may Your anger and wrath turn away from Your city Jerusalem...Therefore, our God, hear the prayer and petitions of Your servant. Show Your favor to Your desolate sanctuary for the Lord's sake...For we are not presenting our petitions before You based on our righteous acts, but based on Your abundant compassion. Lord, hear! Lord, forgive! Lord, listen and act! (Daniel 9:16-19).

> Prayer ebbs and flows with the tide of the Holy Spirit's leading.

Notice how Daniel's petition is based on who God is and what He has done for His people in the past. When Daniel brings his petition to God, he isn't bringing a random, baseless request. Daniel's request for God's anger to subside and His favor to be restored is predicated on the established attributes of God. God is righteous and compassionate, full of justice and mercy. Since it's in God's nature to forgive and restore, Daniel's petition is based on and aimed toward the character of God.

The order of RAP isn't written in stone. When we read all of Daniel 9, we see Daniel devotes most of his prayer to admission; he confesses the sins of the people. In Ezra's prayer, we also see a lot of time devoted to the admission of the people's sins, but we see a rearrangement in order. The prayer in Ezra 9 begins with admission and then moves to recognition and petition. Prayer ebbs and flows with the tide of the Holy Spirit's leading.

In Nehemiah 9, we see how Nehemiah devotes most of his prayer to recognition, praising God for who He is and what He's done on the part of His people in the past. Beginning with the calling of Abram, their deliverance from slavery in Egypt, their provision in the desert, and their inheritance in the Promised Land, Nehemiah's prayer is like a recap of Israel's history. Then he moves to petition the same way Daniel did. Based on all the ways God has worked on their behalf in the past, Nehemiah petitions for God to move on their behalf again to restore Jerusalem.

We can pray the same way, which is why I'm such a big proponent of writing down our prayers.

A Prayer Journal

The prayers I remember the most tend to be the ones I'm still waiting to be answered, for that's where my focus usually lies—on the here and now. I'm inclined to forget the many prayers God has already answered. To do a better job of remembering, after spending time in God's Word, I respond in written prayer. I pour out my heart to God in my journal.

> When we're intentional about remembering God's faithfulness, we can readily proclaim His goodness.

In my own prayers, I want to follow the examples of Daniel and Ezra and Nehemiah. Before I list my petitions, I want to focus first on who God is and all the ways He's already moved in my life. I tell Him all the things I'm thankful for, all the things I notice Him doing. I also tell Him about what's on my heart. God wants us to go to Him with whatever is pressing on us.

When I go back and read my earlier prayers, I realize how God has already moved in certain areas, which gives me all the more reason to give thanks. A prayer journal is a concrete way to remember the deeds of the Lord and consider all His works. When we're

intentional about remembering His faithfulness, we can readily proclaim His goodness.

For me, a prayer journal is one of the dearest ways of communing with God. He loves to communicate through His Word, and
He loves it when we share with Him our thoughts about the passage
we've just read. He loves it, too, when we tell Him about our daily
experiences. Yes, God already knows everything, but He's a rela-
tional God who enjoys spending time with
us. And the more time we spend with Him,
the more we discover how much we truly
enjoy it too.

> Prayer is like
> pulling up a
> chair to talk
> with a Friend.

Whether or not you write down your
prayers, the benefits of prayer are real.

Through Prayer God Helps Us...

1. *Draw closer to Him.* Prayer is like pulling up a chair to
   talk with a Friend, but God isn't just a casual friend.
   He's the all-powerful Maker of the universe, and by His
   amazing grace we can approach the throne of God with
   boldness.[3] When we draw near to God, He will draw
   near to us.[4]

2. *Fix our focus.* When I give my attention to a problem,
   it grows larger in my field of vision. When I give my
   attention to God, He grows larger in my field of vision
   while that problem I was worried about shrinks like a
   petty shadow. Through prayer God adjusts our focus on
   what's eternal and what really matters.

3. *Align our will with God's will.* When we bring competing
   desires into God's presence, He has a way of sorting all

that out. Scripture promises that God will give us a new heart[5] and He'll fill that new heart with His desires.[6]

4. *Deepen our understanding of who God is.* Understanding God doesn't happen through a formula or a checklist of things we need to do; rather, God chooses to reveal Himself through His Word and time in prayer.

5. *See where we need to change.* When we're in His presence, the Holy Spirit shows us the areas in our lives where we need to confess and, in many cases, make healthier choices. God's desire for us is holiness, so He'll show us the areas where we need to grow.

6. *Fortify our hearts and minds.* That comment from a coworker that rubs you raw? That promotion you thought you'd earned? That invitation you didn't receive? That outfit that no longer fits? We wrestle with life's everyday disappointments and hurts in countless ways, but when we pray God becomes a shield and a protector. And those typical frustrations have less and less impact on our hearts and minds.

7. *Know a steadfastness and a peace.* Prayer usually means we've taken a time-out. Even better, we've stopped talking and started listening. God promises to provide a peace we can't describe—because it's other-worldly.[7] While God's peace can't be described, it can be experienced.

The benefits of prayer are many, whether we write in a prayer journal or not. Writing prayers isn't "required," after all. Some days I'm tempted to skip it. And some days are definitely busier than others. But one year I had an experience that forever changed the way I pray.

A friend gave me a journal as a Christmas gift, and that journal ended up holding all my prayers for the next year, from January through December. Then on December 31, I sat down and read my prayer journal from beginning to end—an entire year of prayers, wrapped in the binding of gifted pages, filled with my own handwriting. I had never done this before.

I wept with the turn of each page. Because I'd forgotten already. In just a few short months I'd forgotten some of the ups and downs of that year and how I'd taken them to God in prayer. I'd forgotten how He met me there and comforted me with His presence amid those situations. And I'd forgotten the many, many ways He'd answered those prayers.

> God answers prayer! Most often He answers prayer with Himself.

God answers prayer, my friends. The answer may not come in time for the following Thursday morning prayer meeting. And the answer might not take the form we were looking for and hoping for. But He answers prayer! Most often He answers prayer with Himself. He comes and sits with us. If I hadn't gone back to reread a year's worth of prayers, I would have missed so many of the answers that came through, all in God's perfect timing.

Now I set aside a day at the end of each year to read through my prayer journals. I say *journals*—plural!—because these days I'm filling up three or four of them in just 12 months. And I look forward to December 31, as a day set apart when I can be still and listen to all the ways God has shown Himself present and mighty in my everyday world.

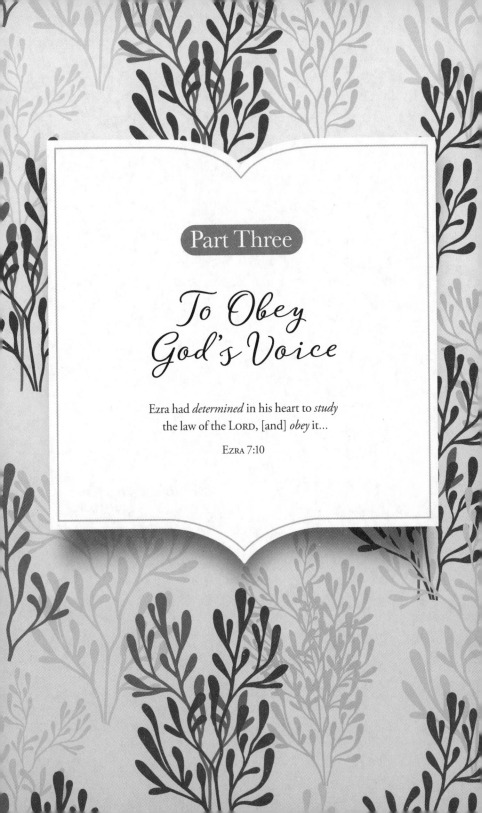

Part Three

To Obey God's Voice

Ezra had *determined* in his heart to *study*
the law of the LORD, [and] *obey* it...

EZRA 7:10

10

The Truth We Live

Obey my voice, and I will be your God, and you shall be my people.

JEREMIAH 7:23 ESV

In the beginning lots of people came. People I knew and people I wondered how my parents knew. As the days and weeks wore on, the visitors came to the hospital less and less, and a new fury smoldered inside me. How can people go about their lives as if others aren't dying? As if some people aren't struggling to breathe? Or can't even walk on their own two feet?

When I returned to school everyone asked how my brother was doing. My friends, my teachers, even my principal. At first I appreciated their concern, but then time moved on. Weeks later I wondered if anyone remembered. Part of me sat in a sixth-grade classroom solving math problems like everyone else while another part of me inhabited the presence of suffering. I didn't have a word for the dissonance I felt. It was a problem I didn't know how to solve.

The sanctuary overflows with people scrunched into every pew, so I climb the stairs and find a seat in the front row of the balcony. Leaning forward I hold the ledge before me and watch the people below me. This is no ordinary church service. I've been waiting for this event all year, where more than 2000 pastors and missionaries gather for an annual convention. Every person here is either in full-time ministry or in a lay-leadership position.

I'm barely out of high school but I want to serve, and youth ministry seems the most logical place. When the music begins, the most notable ministers among us take their seats on stage while the assistant superintendent approaches the podium. We stand to sing, and the hymnals, I notice, are not required. Everyone knows the words by heart.

While we're singing "How Great Thou Art," a man at the end of a pew on the main floor collapses, his body splayed across the aisle. His face glows an ominous crimson, his limbs motionless. A white-haired woman rushes to him. I recognize her immediately. I don't know her, but I know her kind. She moves swiftly, knowing exactly what to do. She assesses whether or not he's breathing, loosens his tie, unbuttons the top of his shirt, and begins chest compressions.

Seeing the commotion, the assistant superintendent waves for the orchestra to stop. From my bird's-eye view it's obvious the people sitting in the back can't tell what's happening. So the man with the microphone explains that a man has fallen and asks the congregation to pray for our brother in need.

A few minutes later everyone shouts "Amen!" and then silence falls. We watch for any sign of movement. Nothing. Several men attempt to carry him out, but he's too large. And the white-haired woman, still pushing on his chest with one fist over the other, insists they leave him alone. So we wait in awkward stillness and wonder if death is in our midst.

From the podium the assistant superintendent assures us someone has called 9-1-1. He pauses and shuffles his feet, as if searching for something else to say. Then he suggests we continue with the announcements while we wait for the paramedics to arrive. He talks about the wonderful work happening all over the world—wells being dug, orphans being fed, souls being saved. Such announcements would normally bring applause, but we're hesitant to clap at the moment.

No paramedics yet.

Now it's time to pray before the offering. The ushers gather at the front, wearing a dubious expression. With another "Amen!" they turn to the pews and pass the offering plates. The orchestra's upbeat offertory painfully contrasts the mood in the room. I watch in disbelief as an offering plate is passed from one person to the next, straight down the row that leads toward the man on the floor. It's like a game of hot potato as they pass the plate as quickly as possible, like Pilate washing his hands to rid himself of this indecency.

The offering plate reaches the end of the row where the man we're not sure is even breathing lies on the floor. His wife is next to him, crying. No one moves except the one lady still doing chest compressions. The man holding the offering plate looks embarrassed and confused until someone from the other side of the aisle reaches for it. They stretch out their arms and pass the offering plate right over the unconscious man.

My fists clamp tight around the ledge. I feel as though I'm back in the sixth grade, when everyone was acting as though everything was fine when nothing was fine at all and I wasn't sure it ever would be again. I want to scream. Why are we continuing as though nothing is happening? A man is probably dying. Right here among us. And we're taking an offering?

God, help us.

A parable comes to mind. The one where a man was beaten and left for dead beside the road. Jesus said a priest passed by on the other side to avoid getting involved. A priest, no less. And here we are—more than 2000 pastors and missionaries under one roof—and we're so inconvenienced by this poor man's demise. The program takes precedence over the person.

I feel as though I should do something, but I'm not sure what I can do. I must be the youngest person present, the least of everyone here. Why would anyone listen to me?

God, please intervene.

From the back of the sanctuary an elderly man begins walking down the center aisle. His silver hair and wrinkled face belie his inner strength, for his gait reveals a man of determination and purpose. When he reaches the front, he looks at the assistant superintendent on stage and says, "I don't mean to interrupt the service, but I believe it has already been interrupted, and I think we should continue praying for our brother."

> It takes courage to stand and walk through a crowd that might not like what you have to say.

A murmur of assent follows.

Everyone stands to pray. Again. Only this time it's more than a perfunctory prayer. No one leads this prayer from a microphone on stage; rather, the voices of men and women join together. Interceding. We lose all track of time. The paramedics arrive and carry the man out on a stretcher. We're not told his condition—if he's alive or dead—but we don't stop praying.

Jesus defined a neighbor as an outsider who rolled up his sleeves, unafraid of the scandal that might ensue if he helped someone lying half dead on the side of the road—someone labeled by society as "unclean." We refer to this story as "The Good Samaritan," for the Samaritan did a good deed. But I don't think it's enough to call him good. He was more than simply good. He was also brave. It takes courage to do the right thing when it means going against the status quo and risking your own reputation to help someone in need.

It also takes courage to stand and walk through a crowd that might not like what you have to say. To call an ambivalent people to prayer. The elder missionary at the convention never yelled or spoke with disdain. He was peaceful yet purposeful, meek yet determined. He was both good *and* brave. And he became my hero that day. I believe he was being obedient to what God had put on his heart to do,

> It's no surprise that Jesus summarized all of God's commands in two: Love God and love others.

and I want to emulate that kind of obedience and courage in my life.

Two major obstacles hinder us from determining in our hearts to follow God. The first is when a tragic event permanently alters our lives for the worse and we feel abandoned by God. The second is when we are hurt, disillusioned, or betrayed by God's people.

It's no surprise that Jesus summarized all of God's commands in two: Love God and love others.[1] For a long time I struggled to love God when He allowed so much heartache in my family, especially in my brother's life. But once I made peace with God and learned to trust Him, I found myself struggling with the second greatest command, to love others.

It's easy to lambast the pastors and missionaries who remained quiet, glued to their pews, while another lay dying in their midst. You probably have your own stories of ghastly moments when a religious leader (or a whole room of them!) failed in some way. We are never short on examples of the many ways God's people have failed—and *continue* to fail. We can easily use every example as evidence of why we don't want to follow God and obey His commands. Not when His people are so flawed.

The repeated failures of His people are ready-made excuses for refusing to obey God's voice. It's the age-old accusation of how the church is full of hypocrites, saying they love God while doing the opposite of what He commands in Scripture. The same accusation has been made for thousands of years.

Before Ezra arrived with the second caravan of exiles, the exiles from the first caravan had grown complacent. They rebuilt the temple altar so the daily sacrifices could resume, as well as the temple foundation, but they didn't finish what they started. Their attention turned inward—wanting bigger, more beautiful homes for themselves. Yet these were the Hebrews willing to leave Babylon and risk the journey across a dangerous desert. These were the ones who *chose* to return home. This was God's remnant!

> We can be believers who not only study God's truth, but also live it.

So God sends the old prophet Haggai to deliver a message to the governor of Jerusalem and the high priest. "Why are you living in luxurious houses while [God's] house lies in ruins?"[2]

God's people had messed up. Big time. They quit working on the temple to build homes for themselves, and not your average dwellings either, but *luxurious* homes. Not everything was as it should be in Jerusalem. If newspapers or blogs had been around back then, reporters and bloggers alike would have thrown the people in Jerusalem under the proverbial bus. We expect more from God's people. They're the ones who should know better, right?

It's no different today. God's people fail. We all do. We may start out with good intentions, but somewhere along the way we get distracted and turn our attention inward. We grow complacent and become self-focused. Rather than doing what's right, we prefer to go along with the crowd.

God, help us.

We can spurn the people in Jerusalem who quit working on the temple, just as we can turn up our noses at the pastors and missionaries who carried on as if a man wasn't suffering in their midst. Or we can choose to be like the elder missionary from the back of the sanctuary or like Haggai in Jerusalem. We can be believers who not only study God's truth, but live it.

When we think of obedience, we tend to think of obligation. We associate obedience with duty, perhaps even drudgery. Nobody enjoys being told what to do. From the earliest age we resist those in authority, like our parents, and we insist on getting our own way. It's our human nature—or more accurately, our sinful nature. Most of us have witnessed the tantrum of a two-year-old, demanding to have her way. Sadly, we also witness adult versions of similar tantrums. I am no different. Sometimes I want what I want, and I resent anybody or anything that stands in my way. But that's not how I want to live.

Obeying God's commands sounds straightforward enough. We might sum it up with the old Nike slogan: Just Do It. If God said

it, then just do it. Obedience, however, is more than sheer determination and grit. Obedience to God's Word requires more than a
"try harder" attitude. This was the purpose of the Mosaic Law in the
Old Testament. The Law was a standard none could achieve. That
was the point. Total obedience wasn't possible. It still isn't. We need
a Savior.

When we go back to the garden of Eden, we see that God gave
Adam and Eve one rule. Not ten, as Moses gave the Israelites. Not
two, as Jesus gave His followers. One. *Do not eat of the tree of knowledge of good and evil.* God didn't tell Adam and Eve to love Him or
serve Him or worship Him. He expected only one thing: their obedience. Because obedience would demonstrate their love, their service, and their worship. [3]

Obedience in a perfect garden in the presence of a holy God
couldn't have been drudgery, but only the sweetest delight. The presence of that one tree, as mentioned earlier, wasn't there to torture
them or tempt them. God placed it there to give Adam and Eve free
will. They could choose whether to obey God or not. Their motivation for eating from the one forbidden tree was an echo of doubt, of
mistrust, that God was holding out on them. That's what the snake
told them. And so they ate. They wanted more than what they
already had. They wanted to experience for themselves whatever it
was God didn't want them to taste.

> The motivation
> for Christ's
> obedience was
> love. I want my
> obedience to be
> out of love too.

Through Adam and Eve's disobedience
sin entered the world. Humanity has been
struggling under the strain of sin ever since,
but through Jesus's obedience we've been
reconciled with God, our relationship with
Him restored.

He humbled Himself by becoming obedient to the point
of death—even to death on a cross (Philippians 2:8).

Now, if obedience could ever be described as drudgery, surely
this is it. Death by crucifixion is the definition of excruciating pain,
but the writer of Hebrews says that for the joy set before Him, Jesus
endured the cross.[4] This doesn't mean the cross itself was a joy;
rather, He *endured* the cross because of the joy that waited on the
other side—being reunited with the people He so dearly loves.

The motivation for Christ's obedience was love. I want my obedience to be out of love too. More often than not, I think it is, but I
still have days when I bite my lower lip and step forward in obedience while secretly hoping somebody notices the sacrifice I'm making. I know when I'm doing the right thing for the wrong reason,
because that's when I want credit for it. When I'm doing the right
thing with a right heart, I'm content my Father knows and nobody
else. That's enough for me. Because He's enough.

Part One of this book addresses the question *Why should I choose to follow God in the
face of so much heartache?* Part Two addresses
the question *How should I study God's Word?*
Part Three now addresses the question *How
can I live with a heart of obedience to God's
Word?* The hurdles we face are many. None
more so than the plain fact that obedience
might cost us something. At least, some-
thing in the here and now. Yet our obedience to God always reaps
something beautiful and bountiful, whether we see that beauty and
bounty here in this life or later.

> When we
> obey with a
> right heart, we
> experience a joy
> and peace we'd
> never know
> otherwise.

When we obey with a right heart, from a place of love, we experience a joy and peace we'd never know otherwise. It's important,

though, that we never mistake our obedience to God's Word—or the good deeds we do—for our right to enter eternity in God's presence. That passageway was secured by Christ's obedience, not ours. Our obedience is simply the natural outgrowth of a life yielded to Christ.

The church in Galatia got this backward, so the apostle Paul had to straighten them out. The Galatians thought salvation was acquired through Jesus *plus* the observance of certain Jewish rituals. They wanted to hook their ticket to heaven to some of their own doing. That way they could take a little bit of credit for their salvation. But Paul adamantly denied this teaching. He called it a false gospel.[5] Our obedience doesn't grant our access to heaven; our obedience is how we become more like Christ.

This is why studying God's Word is foundational to becoming more like Christ. It's through His Word we learn to recognize God's voice, and it's through the Holy Spirit living inside us as believers that we're enabled to walk in obedience. Studying the Bible for the sake of information is never the goal. We study the Bible to be transformed. And as we become living testimonies of God's life-changing truth and grace, we reach those around us with the good news that transformation is possible for them too.

11

The Compass We Follow

*Show me the right path, O LORD; point
out the road for me to follow.*

PSALM 25:4-5 NLT

I watched in fascination as Kendall rolled each article of clothing
tight and stuffed it into his backpack. He tucked pouches of dried
food in there, too, along with a condensed roll of toilet paper. Kendall and Dad were planning a campout, but their campsite couldn't
be reached by vehicle. They planned to hike most of one day just to
reach their destination, and the only food available would be what
they carried with them or the fish they caught in a stream. Kendall
called this "real camping."

While my brother packed everything he needed to survive a week
in the wild, I tinkered with his metal compass. No matter which
way I turned it or tilted it, the needle's arrow pointed in the same
direction—north.

Kendall said his compass was the most important thing he'd
need with him because there were no signs where they were going.
Part of me wanted to go with them on their adventure, but Dad said
I was too little. Another part of me was glad to stay home, though,
because they said it would get cold at night.

Within a few short years those hiking trips came to an end. Faraway places over rocks and streams can't be reached by wheelchair.

Up and down the street church members gather for a peaceful demonstration. It looks as though everyone from my church is here, and people from other churches are here too. In a show of solidarity, churches across denominations have banded together for this outdoor event. Hundreds of churchgoers line two main streets that run perpendicular to each other. The idea is for us to stand on the sidewalk in the formation of a cross at one of the most prominent intersections in the city.

For weeks now we've been hearing about this demonstration. Our purpose, we're told, is to declare truth in a peaceful manner. That's all. I'm in my late teens, and I'm eager to join the adult activities at church, so I go along with the plan. We're not to say anything. Just hold a sign. Each person. Shoulder to shoulder. Toe to curb. And quietly pray for each passerby.

But something about the whole thing unsettles me. Our signs say ABORTION IS MURDER in red capital letters. The pastors, however, get to hold different signs that say GOD FORGIVES in green capital letters. As I look around I see red signs everywhere. Every few hundred or so, a lone green sign dots the landscape.

Cars honk at us, but I can't tell if they're happy honks or mad honks. Some people roll down their windows and give us a thumbs-up. Other people roll down their windows and give us the middle finger. A pastor holding a green-letter sign walks behind our line, whispering to those of us with red-letter signs, "Remember to pray. We're here to be peaceful. Turn the other cheek. Don't shout back."

I try to pray for the people in the cars, but it's not the noisy cars that draw my attention. It's the quiet ones. While some folks drive by and express hostility, others refuse to look at us. They keep their eyes fixed straight ahead as they drive past all our red-laden signs.

When the traffic light at a nearby intersection turns red, a car has to stop right in front of me. A girl in the passenger seat, not much older than me, stares at something ahead. Her face is void of any emotion. Empty. Expressionless.

The deadness in her eyes grips me. Could she be guilty of the red letters? If so, what combination of tragic circumstances led her to such a fateful end? I lower my sign and look at her intently. I want her to see compassion on my face and know my heart's intent. I pray for God to turn her eyes toward mine. I'm not here to judge anyone, but my sign indicates otherwise. The red letters in my hands have become an uncrossable barrier between me and the girl with dead eyes.

I wish I had one of those green signs, for in this moment perhaps what she really needs is a thousand green signs. A thousand times a thousand times a thousand. GOD FORGIVES. GOD FORGIVES. GOD FORGIVES.

A deep conviction overwhelms me. Several of my friends are standing close by and one of them is wearing a WWJD bracelet: "What would Jesus do?" The bracelet reminds us to consider how Jesus would respond in any given situation.

> His first words are full of grace. *Neither do I condemn you.* His next words are full of truth. *From now on sin no more.*

Except we don't have to speculate. The Gospel of John tells us. When the most dedicated church leaders, the Pharisees, bring a woman who's been caught in adultery to Jesus, they question Him about the law. It's clear they don't care about her. They're only using her to trap Jesus with the "truth" of the law so they can find an excuse to arrest Him. The law said adultery was punishable by death, so they push and push until finally Jesus answers them, "Let the one who has never sinned throw the first stone!"[1]

One by one the church leaders walk away. Did Jesus neglect the truth of the law? Not at all. He asks her where her accusers are, if any of them have condemned her. She can't do anything but shrug her shoulders. None of the church leaders have condemned her, and she tells Him so. And here's the best part:

> Jesus said, "Neither do I. Go and sin no more (John 8:11 NLT).

His first words are full of grace. Neither do I condemn you. His next words are full of truth. From now on sin no more.[2]

What would Jesus do if He were standing on this curb with me? I can't imagine Him casting red-lettered stones at random. He'd point out that we're all sinners in desperate need of grace. That's the message I want to share. I don't want to pick on one particular sin and herald it as somehow worse than my own. We're all sinners. And I want to reach the woman in pain—the one who's caught in what feels like an impossible situation—as much as I want to protect the life she carries inside her. But calling her a murderer? That won't reach her. Why would she ever want to step foot inside a church full of people who choose to spend an afternoon calling people names because of their sin?

Jesus says anyone who's angry with someone will be subject to judgment the same as the one who is guilty of murder.[3] Basically, He raises the bar. Because as soon as we're tempted to pat ourselves on the back and think of ourselves as better than another person for not committing a certain sin, that's when the sin of pride chokes our own souls.

The light turns green and the girl never looks my way. Another car honks. This time it's a thumbs-up. I shake my head and silently pray: *Father, forgive us, for we know not what we do.*

I turn around and walk to my car.

More than 25 years have passed since I stood on that curb and held that red-letter sign, and it grieves me every time I think about it. The topic of abortion is sensitive and oftentimes divisive, but my point here is not a political one. I'm not poking at parochial establishments either. I have no doubt that most of the people standing on that sidewalk had the same intentions I did. We followed the direction of our leaders because we believe in the sanctity of life, but I'm no longer convinced this is the wisest, nor kindest, way to communicate this truth. I'm pointing fingers at myself here, because that moment—when I yearned to give hope to a girl with lifeless eyes—served as a critical juncture in my life. I needed a compass.

Whenever we're not sure how to respond in a given situation, we can't exactly stop and read the entire Bible right there on the spot. Besides, the Bible isn't an almanac or an encyclopedia where we look up the specific information we want and leave the rest. But the Bible does provide the guidance we need. By reading it daily we internalize God's truth and we learn to recognize the character of His voice. Not audibly, but textually. It's there in the fabric of the words on each page.

> As followers of Christ we're pilgrims on this earth, journeying together to become more like Jesus, full of grace and truth.

As we read the Bible, we grow in our understanding of who He is because He always responds in a way that's consistent with His character. Then, when a question arises, the Holy Spirit brings to mind what we've previously read.

More specifically, Jesus's words to the woman caught in adultery illustrate the compass we need when we're wondering how to move forward in obedience. When John recorded this story in his Gospel account, he had already established the foundation for this compass a few chapters earlier when he said Jesus came from the Father "full of grace and truth" (1:14).

The guiding principle in my life—my pocket-ready compass for obedience—comes from John 1:14. Jesus wasn't 50 percent grace and 50 percent truth. He was full of both.[4] And if we're to be like Christ, we should be too.

> In our brokenness we tend to fall to one side or the other. We tend to be natural Grace Givers or natural Truth Tellers.

As followers of Christ we're pilgrims on this earth, journeying together to become more like Jesus, full of grace and truth. In our brokenness we tend to fall to one side or the other. We tend to be natural Grace Givers or natural Truth Tellers. I'm a Truth Teller, but I've been on a journey of growing in grace too. I want my thoughts, words, and deeds to be full of grace and truth in the likeness of Jesus Christ. Whenever I'm not sure how to respond in a given situation, I ask myself, *Is what I'm saying or doing consistent with God's truth? Am I communicating God's truth with grace?* Pastor Randy Alcorn calls this a "two-point checklist of Christlikeness."[5] This two-point checklist makes a reliable compass when we need to know the path we should take.

Before the Babylonians invaded Jerusalem and carted off the surviving Israelites into captivity, the prophet Jeremiah gave warning after warning. He preached the truth and pleaded for the people to turn back to God. Jeremiah knew what was coming and he lived to see the destruction with his own eyes. Today he's most known for saying,

If my head were a spring of water, my eyes a fountain of tears, I would weep day and night over the slain of my dear people (Jeremiah 9:1).

Jeremiah is dubbed the weeping prophet, and his nickname teaches us an important lesson. God didn't choose a hard man to tell a hard truth.[6] God appointed a prophet who would share in the heartache of the truth he faithfully delivered. The truth came with tears. Jeremiah spoke the truth in a spirit of grace.

Whenever we have a hard truth to tell, may we pray until our hearts are flooded with tear-filled grace.

The more we read the Bible, the more we see God's grace and truth throughout the totality of Scripture. When Ezra prayed for the remnant in Jerusalem, he acknowledged their exile as judgment from God's hand of

> Truth without grace is extreme legalism. Grace without truth is extreme liberalism.

truth, and he recognized their restoration as mercy from God's hand of grace.

> Our guilt has been terrible from the days of our fathers until the present. Because of our iniquities we have been handed over, along with our kings and priests, to the surrounding kings, and to the sword, captivity, plundering, and open shame, as it is today. But now, for a brief moment, grace has come from Yahweh our God to preserve a remnant for us and give us a stake in His holy place (Ezra 9:7-8).

This is the God we serve. A God of both grace and truth.

God's people, however, tend to embrace one over the other, and many churches do the same. It's common to find Truth Tellers going to church together and Grace Givers going to church together. It's more comfortable that way. The problem is, to be like Christ we need both. Truth without grace is extreme legalism. Grace without truth is extreme liberalism.[7] Yet the fullness of both grace and truth is essential to living like our Lord.

> When we're immersed in the grace and truth of Jesus Christ, we find the path that leads us home.

I recently watched my husband, Jeff, and our son, Parker, prepare for a camping trip. Their packing list included a compass. It's fancier than the one Kendall had. This compass has a metal hook so Parker can latch it around the belt loop on his pants. It lights up, too, so you can read it at night. But like all compasses, it still does that thing when you turn it around or upside down. The arrow points due north. Always. And that's what Scripture does for us. When we're immersed in the grace and truth of God's Word, we find the path that leads us home.

12

The Failure We Grieve

*When you pass through the waters, I will be with you;
and when you pass through the rivers, they will not sweep over you.*

Isaiah 43:2 NIV

I was born and raised in Northern California, but I've lived in Southern California now for two decades. The drive back home takes about eight hours, depending on how often I stop along the way. I've made the trip many times, but every one brings up memories. Many of which I'd rather forget.

When Ezra wrote about leading the second caravan of exiles from Babylon to Jerusalem, he made little mention of the trip, which is surprising because he kept fastidious records of everything. Record-keeping was likely his job in Babylon, yet the journey itself—from exile to home—received few words in the annals of Scripture.

> [Ezra] began the journey from Babylon on the first day of the first month and arrived in Jerusalem on the first day of the fifth month since the gracious hand of his God was on him (Ezra 7:9).

That's it. One day they're in Babylon and four months later they're in Jerusalem. Ezra saves his words for the restoration of Jerusalem and their new way of life, but I'm interested to know what the journey was like. Did the people experience joy and anticipation?

Maybe a little fear of the unknown? Was anyone born along the way? Wouldn't that be a story to tell!

This is the plight of every writer. What to leave in and what to leave out. Ezra left out the details of their travel. He must not have thought they were important, or perhaps he had other reasons. I've shared a little about my early years, wandering hospital hallways while struggling to trust a God who allows so much suffering. I've also shared about my later years, teaching in classrooms while doing life with my family. But until now I've omitted a portion of years, between my teens and my thirties and beyond. I call my twenties "the dark decade." When most people my age were living in dorms or starting careers or getting together on Thursday nights to watch an episode of *Friends*, I walked a lonely, painful road.

In all my years of blogging I've never written about this season of my life, and I rarely talk about it in person except with those closest to me. But every now and then I find myself in a conversation, face-to-face with a friend, and I sense the Lord prompting me to share this part of my story. I sense that same prompting now. This book is about determining in our hearts to study God's Word and obey God's voice because, when we do, we're set free from the brokenness that binds us and the sinful patterns that permeate our choices. I believe this in the marrow of my soul because I've known the heartache that inevitably comes from disobedience.

The psalmist is right when he says one day in God's courts is better than a thousand elsewhere.[1] I've lived in elsewhere, and I promise you it leads to nowhere good.

I never took the SAT exam in high school. As soon as I graduated from high school, I began working full-time, but then I did something crazy. I drove to a local community college and signed up for some classes. I'm not sure what gave me such a bold idea. Maybe it was the sight of my brother wheeling across a football field to receive the first college diploma on either side of our family. Kendall has always inspired me to do more than my limitations might impose.

A few weeks into my first semester, however, my work schedule changed and I had to withdraw from my classes. My first college report card had a line of *W*'s straight down the page. But I signed up again the following semester and prayed my work schedule wouldn't change.

Then something else changed.

I got married when I was 19 and my husband's job moved us 400 miles away. I enrolled at a new community college and began the process all over, but his job ended up changing four times in the first five years of our marriage. Each job meant another move, another city, and another community college. If I was lucky I'd get to finish the semester before having to move again.

By the time I was 24, I was the mother of a sweet two-year-old daughter and finally able to transfer to a Christian university in Southern California. I was beyond excited, but when I arrived, I didn't fit in. My fellow students were fresh out of high school and living in dorms while I commuted to campus. They probably thought it was weird that a fellow student was a wife and a mom. I was in a new city, again, without friends and plagued with self-doubt. *Will I ever finish?*

Being new to the area, I found a church and joined the choir. But then my world turned upside down as the word *divorce* became a reality—something I never planned or thought would be a part of my life. Nobody at church knew my story because I didn't tell them.

I didn't like the way my story was going, and deep down I hoped and prayed it would all get turned around before I'd have to admit to anyone how bad things had really become. So I kept wearing my wedding ring to keep up appearances.

> Fear and shame swirled around me like a tornado, creating an impenetrable force, keeping everyone at a distance.

In choir we were usually busy singing and didn't have much time to talk, which was fine with me. Talking was risky. Conversations could lead to questions and questions could lead to disclosures. Perhaps a professional—or even an outside observer—would have been able to see I was in denial. Talking about something makes it real, and I desperately didn't want this to be real. So I kept quiet.

On Sunday mornings the choir sang in two services, and between the services the other choir members gathered around donuts and coffee backstage while I found a quiet corner to be alone and read my Bible. This may have looked spiritual of me on the outside, but on the inside I was running from the truth of my own life. Fear and shame swirled around me like a tornado, creating an impenetrable force, keeping everyone at a distance. This was never supposed to be me.

I felt like the woman at the well who fetched her water at midday when she knew no one else would be there. She knew everyone in the village drew their water first thing in the morning. Given her questionable history, she was probably avoiding awkward conversations. I could relate.

While sitting in my self-imposed corner one Sunday, I sensed God telling me to read Isaiah, which was weird because I normally avoided the prophetic books. So I tried to bargain with God. *How about some history? Or poetry? Or a New Testament epistle?*

God's voice was clear. *Isaiah.*

Whenever I'm not sure if I've really heard God's voice, I ask three questions:

One: Does it align with God's Word? In this case, it was cut-and-dried. Reading the book of Isaiah couldn't be counter to the commands in Scripture. So I looked to the other two indicators.

Two: Would this thought have occurred to me on my own? You know, like the thought that I should get in my car at 8:30 at night, even though I'm already wearing pajamas, and go through the Taco Bell drive-thru for a Burrito Supreme. Yeah, I could come up with that on my own, and sometimes do. But when a thought occurs to me I know could never have originated with me, I pay attention.

In this case, I never would have come up with the idea to read Isaiah on my own. That book is 66 chapters of prophecy! I didn't understand much of it the first time I read it, so I wasn't sure what good it would do now. Besides, if the thought didn't originate with me, and if it didn't originate with God, the only other alternative would be that it originated with the devil, but that's preposterous. Why would the devil want me to read the Bible at all? If he wanted to entice me, surely he could come up with something better than "Read Isaiah."

Three: Do I have peace if I refuse? There's something so steadfast about being in God's will that I know when I've stepped out of it. A deep, inner peace—something that's hard to describe but always present—leaves. In its place a wrestling begins. Another telltale sign shows up too. I begin to rationalize all the reasons I shouldn't do what I think God is asking me to do. Did I mention Isaiah is prophecy? And that it wouldn't do me any good to read it since I already knew I didn't understand it? I was happy to read my Bible, but how about 1 and 2 Samuel? Or the Psalms? Esther? Luke? Romans? I'd be willing to read Job again if it meant avoiding Isaiah.

I flipped open my Bible and read a psalm, but that same inner wrestling continued until I reluctantly turned to Isaiah. I couldn't imagine a prophet from thousands of years ago having anything to say that would be of value or comfort, but I read the first chapter of Isaiah anyway, half hoping something revelatory would happen. Nothing. When the choir lined up to sing for the second service, I was relieved to be done with Isaiah. At least for that week.

Sunday after Sunday I sang in the choir, and in between services I continued to sit alone in my corner, reading a couple more chapters in Isaiah. One Sunday I settled into my familiar corner and opened my Bible to the next chapter waiting, Isaiah 54. But I couldn't read. Not anymore. I was too weary. I knew it was more than the full-time job and the night classes and the single-parenting that was exhausting me. It was the charade.

Too soul-weary to continue, I bowed my head and confessed: *God, I'm so afraid of what people will think when they find out I'm going through a divorce. I'm so ashamed. I just can't bring myself to tell anyone.*

I let out a heavy sigh, unsure of what else to do but return to my ritual reading. Then I read these words by Isaiah:

> "Do not be afraid; you will not be put to shame. Do not fear disgrace; you will not be humiliated. You will forget the shame of your youth and remember no more the reproach of your widowhood. For your Maker is your husband—the LORD Almighty is his name—the Holy One of Israel is your Redeemer; he is called the God of all the earth. The LORD will call you back as if you were a wife deserted and distressed in spirit—a wife who married young, only to be rejected," says your God. "For a brief moment I abandoned you, but with deep compassion I will bring you back. In a surge of anger I hid my face from you for a moment, but with everlasting kindness I will have compassion on you," says the LORD your Redeemer (54:4-8 NIV).

Isaiah was speaking to the people of Israel—the ones living in exile. But the timing of this passage, right after my prayer, brought a peace I couldn't describe. I wondered, too, if God was telling me to get honest. To tell someone about my divorce. I was living a lie— wearing my wedding ring and pretending to be married when I wasn't anymore.

I looked up to see the choir getting in line for the second service and joined them, wondering how I wasn't supposed to feel ashamed when deep inside the failure of my marriage was smothering me.

> Was it possible that God literally knocked me off my feet to get me to finally own up to the truth?

While standing on stage, I tried to sing the words of the chorus, but my head turned foggy and my vision blurred. The next thing I knew I was backstage, lying across several chairs. A circle of blue-haired choir ladies surrounded me, saying, "Are you okay, honey?" "Did you have any breakfast this morning?" "Don't worry about it, sweetie, you just passed out, is all. You're probably just pregnant."

What? I sat straight up despite my pounding head. "What happened?"

They said I fainted and a baritone from the back row carried me off stage.

Oh, God, please tell me this isn't true.

I wanted to slither off my chair, melt into the floor, and disappear forever.

Behind the choir ladies, the worship pastor held a phone in his hand. "Denise, what's your phone number? Let me call your husband to come pick you up."

I freeze.

Then I remember the words of Isaiah from less than an hour before...*Do not be afraid; you will not suffer shame.* Something told me I was supposed to be honest. Was it possible that God literally knocked me off my feet to get me to finally own up to the truth?

I took a deep breath and said, "Can I have some water?"

The worship pastor replied, "Oh, right. I'll go get some."

The choir ladies followed him, "We'll get you some food, honey. You just stay there and rest."

> I heard the voice of hope...we serve a God who resurrects the dead and brings new life.

One by one they left. I had chickened out. I couldn't bring myself to tell the truth. But one woman, Juanita, stayed behind with her arm wrapped tight around me while the words of Isaiah kept reverberating through me. *Do not fear disgrace; you will not be humiliated.*

Against my will tears spilled out and I told Juanita, "You can't call home. There's nobody there."

I told her everything, and she just closed her eyes and listened. She never let me go.

When I finished, she shared a story with me. Thirty years earlier her first husband left her. I had no idea. All I knew was a gracious woman married to a lawyer with two amazing teenage children. I knew the after, not the before.

As Juanita told me her story, I heard the voice of hope...There is life after death. This may feel like a death now, but we serve a God who resurrects the dead and brings new life. Trust Him with everything. You'll see.

There I was. Fallen. In the middle of a Sunday morning service. Carried out. Unconscious. So broken I couldn't hide it any longer. But God had not abandoned me. He was right there with me, with the arms of Jesus wrapped tight around me as my sister in Christ whispered hope to a battered and broken soul.

Some people say they don't have regrets. I'm not one of them. My sweet daughter was in preschool when her parents split, and I'll always carry a certain sadness that she grew up in a broken home—in my broken story. She's in college now and an absolute delight to everyone who knows her. The consequences of divorce, however, are real and far-reaching. We know that.

Divorce is the external evidence of an internal brokenness. It's a private pain made public. I know all the verses in the Bible about divorce. I've read every one. It doesn't surprise me that God hates divorce; anyone who's ever been through one hates it too. A divorce is a massive earthquake that happens in the hidden depths of the ocean, sending one tsunami after another until you're swallowed whole, unable to breathe. People can see the tsunamis, but they can't see the fissure that broke your world in two.

In the Bible James is pretty straightforward when he says, "For whoever keeps the entire law, yet fails in one point, is guilty of breaking it all."[2] In other words, it only takes one sin to make us a sinner and it doesn't matter which sin it is. All sin separates us from God, but the natural consequences we endure as a result of our sin will vary. Lying to a friend might wreck a relationship. Lying to a judge might land you in jail.

> Sin is like mold. When it's exposed to light, it can't grow.

Still, there's no denying the fact that divorce is a sin with a social stigma—especially in the church. It's the scarlet *D* you're branded with for the rest of your life. Even the so-called "Welcome Card" at church that asks for your name and email address also asks you to state up front whether you're single, married, widowed, or divorced. I've yet to find a "Welcome Card" at church that asks new visitors to check a box if they've ever lied or cheated or looked at porngraphy. Divorce is the only sin you get labeled with on your very first day at church. The spiritual and emotional segregation is palpable.

To be fair, divorce isn't the kind of sin that just happens one day. It's usually a culmination of many other sins along the way—the lesser-known sins, the ones kept well hidden. Sin is like mold. When it's exposed to light, it can't grow, but when it's allowed to remain in the dark, it grows until it eats away everything healthy and good. When a divorce is announced and everyone is shocked by the news, it means a lot was happening behind the scenes that few people knew anything about. Like the Titanic, the once-strong marriage everyone saw as unsinkable is now broken into halves and unable to stay afloat. The two halves drift apart and succumb to the waters overtaking them. Even worse, the wreckage takes the lives of other innocent people, especially when kids are involved.

The sinking of the actual Titanic was more than just a tragedy because it was completely avoidable.[3] The warning signs were ignored. Eventually, it was not one big impact, or one big hole in the ship that caused it to sink. It was a series of punctures along the starboard side.

In the same way, it's usually not one isolated event or one giant catastrophe that causes a divorce. Rather, it's a series of sins that, if left unchecked, leads toward the breaking of a marriage. This is why a failed marriage is so devastating. It's a public admission that something hadn't been working for a long time. That some things weren't being brought to light.

Every situation is different and, ultimately, a healthy and thriving marriage requires two willing adults. In many cases, one spouse is willing to try but the other has made the divorce decision for them.

In my mid-twenties, when most people my age were finishing college and getting their first "real job," I went through a divorce and became a single mom. When all of this was happening, I sensed the Lord telling me never to speak ill of my daughter's father. In this matter I have strived to be obedient. We were two broken people who failed to make a marriage work, and I take responsibility for my part in the demise. God knows every detail. And on my darkest day in my darkest year, God spoke to me through His Word. Through the words of Isaiah He told me not to be afraid. Just as Isaiah promised the people of Israel that God would one day bring them back from their exile, I heard God saying He'd be faithful to bring me back from my exile.

The failure we grieve will be different for all of us. Perhaps for you it wasn't a divorce. Maybe it was something else. Whatever it was or is or may someday be, the truth of God's grace remains. He's always ready to rescue and save, deliver and redeem. Whatever happened yesterday or last year or a lifetime ago, we can come to Him with all of it.

> Obedience is a matter of moving forward, one step at a time, tethered to God's Word as our guide.

That's what a life of obedience looks like. Not a seamless progression toward perfection, but a heart of repentance that returns to God's path. Obedience is a matter of moving forward, one step at a time, tethered to God's Word as our guide.

13

The Purpose We Reclaim

Then Jonah prayed to the LORD his God from the belly of the fish saying,
"I called out to the LORD, out of my distress, and he answered me...
For you cast me into the deep, into the heart of the seas,
and the flood surrounded me;
all your waves and your billows passed over me...
The waters closed in over me to take my life; the deep surrounded me...
When my life was fainting away, I remembered the LORD,
and my prayer came to you...Salvation belongs to the LORD!"

JONAH 2:1-9 ESV

In near panic, I kick and flail until my face breaks the water's surface. I gasp for air, swallowing hard. My three-year-old daughter can barely swim, so I wrap her arms around my shoulders so she won't drown. A distant light on the shore is our only hope.

I swim with one arm while balancing my little girl above the water with the other. Somehow I find a steady rhythm and we're no longer in immediate danger. We're both breathing, and that's something. Then another fear pushes into my mind. The water bites my skin with unrelenting cold. Even if I'm able to reach the shore, hypothermia could set in for us both. No matter how fast I swim it might not be fast enough. Fear digs its talons into my heart.

God, please help us reach the shore.

I sit up in bed. Panting and sweating. The sheets look as if I've been thrashing about for hours. It's the same nightmare. Every night.

I'm afraid to lie back on my pillow. Any notion of sleep threatens the return of dark waters, so I slip out of bed and onto the floor. My knees are the only way to keep breathing.

God, I'm so afraid. I keep reading statistics about the risks children face while growing up in a single-parent home. Please, God, spare my little girl. Don't let her become a statistic.

I went to the circus once and watched an acrobat fling herself through the air. Another acrobat was always there, on another swing, ready to catch her at the right moment. At the circus I was never worried because a giant net ensured their safety if they fell. But right now I'm worried. I'm worried about my daughter. I'm worried about the rent. And I'm worried about getting a better job. I know I'm not supposed to worry, but I'm living without a net. If I fall, no one is there to catch me. And my daughter is depending on me.

I feel like Peter in the Bible. He knew what life was like without a net because he left a net full of fish—a winning lottery ticket if ever there was one—to follow Jesus. *Then* he failed. And after his failure, Peter found himself fishing again, clinging to an old familiar net. That's when Someone on the shore suggested he and his companions try the other side. The catch was so huge Peter knew it could only be because of the Lord, so he jumped into the water and thrashed his way through dark waves.[1] In that moment he knew one thing: the Light on the shore was his only hope.

Without a college degree the only jobs I can find are through a temp agency. They send me on different assignments every week while my tiny daughter goes to preschool. Being away from her during the day is agony. We've been together 24/7 since the moment she was born. We don't have family nearby to help and now we're apart all day.

I pray for God to make a way for us to be together again, but it feels as though I'm praying for a miracle—the whole notion of which I struggle with. My brother never received a miracle. My marriage didn't either. Despite countless prayers. In my mind, miracles are for stories in the Bible, not for us today.

One evening I rush through Los Angeles traffic to reach the preschool before they close at 6:00. The fees for being late are a constant threat to my meager income. When the preschool director stops me at the door and asks if she can talk to me, my mind races to every worst-case scenario. *Is my daughter hurt? Did I bounce a check?* The director has exactly 2.3 seconds to allay my fears before full-throttle panic sets in.

She smiles and says, "One of our teachers resigned today. Would you be interested in filling her spot?"

> Hope is the only way to survive.

Only God.

For the next two years I work full-time at my daughter's preschool, where she and I can be together. This also allows me to get to know the other moms of preschoolers as they do their dropping off and picking up. Several of them are single moms, too, and we forge new friendships and help each other out whenever we need childcare in the evenings or on weekends. With their help I'm able to continue taking a few college classes at night. All together it would take me ten years of night classes, but eventually, I finish.

When Kendall wakes up from being under general anesthesia for more than 12 hours, he's disoriented and groggy, but when he's fully awake, he realizes he can't feel his legs. And he's told the reality of his fate. His future is in a wheelchair. A few days later he tells Mom he knows what he wants to be when he grows up. Someday he'd like to be a stand-up comic.

My brother becomes the patient every doctor and nurse in the hospital hears about. He's the boy who shouldn't have survived that car accident and the patient who endures unimaginable pain with a contagious hope that spreads through every hall and every room. Because hope is the only way to survive.

To dream of a life better than the one we're living now is the only way to wake up each morning and press forward. The most famous dreamer in the Bible is Joseph, Abraham's great-grandson, whose brothers sell him into slavery. Joseph is carted off to Egypt, where he's forced to learn a new language and serve his captors. It's another story of exile, only this one came before the exile to Babylon.

No matter what Joseph does, things don't work out for him. As a slave he works hard for his master, but then he's falsely accused of attempted rape and ends up in prison. He's misunderstood and mistreated, accused and forgotten. The dreamer never dreamed of living in a prison cell, but through a crazy turn of events, he's later called to interpret a dream for Pharaoh, who then commissions Joseph to serve as second in command in Egypt. When famine hits, as Joseph had predicted, he's responsible for saving everyone's lives, including the lives of his own family. [2]

> The "in between" times in our lives become the crucible where God reshapes us into His likeness.

I've always felt somewhat akin to Joseph. He was a dreamer who spent years between the dreaming and the fruition of his dream. That's where many of us are today. We're in the years in between. Forced into a prison of our own, whether confined to a wheelchair or stuck in a divorce or trapped in poverty or limited in opportunity.

The Bible is replete with people who spent a part of their lives "in between." Moses fled Egypt after killing a man and spent the next 40 years in a desert before he heard the voice of God in a burning bush, telling him to go back to Egypt. His fugitive years became his preparation for another 40 years in the desert, where he would lead the Hebrews on a journey toward the Promised Land.

David spent years fleeing a crazy king who was hell-bent on killing him. He hid in caves and lived hand-to-mouth until the promise of his kingdom became a reality. Those caves became a school for waiting on God.

Even Jonah spent three days imprisoned in the belly of a fish, where he finally relented to God's purpose for his life and prayed to be rescued from deep waters. In a strange paradox, Jonah's captivity became his salvation.

These "in between" times and places become the crucible where God reshapes us into His likeness. Ezra dreamed of returning to Jerusalem to reinstate the temple rituals, to teach God's Word, and to raise up a new generation of scribes to make copies of Scripture. And his time in Babylon prepared him for such a task. His skill as a scribe in Babylon became his greatest asset back in Jerusalem. Ezra knew God's Word better than anyone, and he knew firsthand what could happen when people turn away from God. His exile became his crucible.

> Ezra's exile became his crucible. In the same way, our exile becomes our crucible too.

In the same way, our exile becomes our crucible too.

At choir rehearsal the worship pastor announces the Creative
Arts Ministry is putting together a Broadway-style production of
Joseph and the Amazing Technicolor Dreamcoat. They've even hired
a professional choreographer from Hollywood. And they'd like the
choir to participate. Maybe as extras or something.

The following Saturday I walk into church and find the audito-
rium filled with people, young and old, stretching their limbs and
preparing for a workout. I thought this would be a church-choir
thing, but there are people here I've never seen before. Many of
them brought 8x10 headshots of themselves with their résumé on
the back. I didn't even know that was a thing. When the choreographer begins to teach a dance routine, everyone in the room falls
into place. We're supposed to learn the routine and perform it later
for a panel of judges.

A blizzard of conflicted feelings swirl to the surface. I haven't
danced since I was 12, not since my brother's accident. Moving to
music used to be intrinsic, natural. When words failed me, which
was often, music could reach me in ways nothing else could. I studied ballet for years and started dancing on pointe when I was 11. A
year later my brother's legs quit working and I quit dancing.

To step onto the dance floor after so many years away feels like
the biggest leap of faith I could possibly muster. The choreographer
begins with warm-up exercises, and I remember how much I used
to like this part. The stretching and the balancing. After a while it's
just me and music and movement. This I remember. I remember
my first recital, my first bow, and my first pair of pointe shoes. The
silky ribbon on the outside belies the hard reality on the inside. The
hardness is what allows the dancer to stand on her toes. While pir-
ouettes and arabesques appear a mere flutter of grace to the outside observer, the dancer's feet feel every bruise and blister. A dancer
must hide this truth. The show must go on.

I also remember how the dance never really ends. After I hung up my shoes, I continued through life with smiles and façades, giving an illusion of grace and ease, but hidden within the pain etched deep. I continued this dance, without the satin shoes, for years too long. Then God allowed my circumstances to crumble around me. The pretty dance of life-as-I-knew-it ended. My stark reality remained. Bruised and in need of real grace.

> Here today, a new dance begins. Grace envelopes me. I bow low, yielding in my heart to the One who knows me truest of all.

Here today, a new dance begins. Grace envelopes me. I bow low, yielding in my heart to the One who knows me truest of all. I submit to His will for me. When the music ends, I rise to see the panel of judges before me. I forgot they were there, but they smile and say I'm the newest member of "Joseph's family." And I can't remember the last time I felt so at home.

A few weeks later, I take a seat in the front row of the sanctuary. The next scene is for Joseph and his brothers, so the rest of us can sit and watch. As they rehearse, a huge stage light falls to the floor, spewing shards of glass everywhere. If anyone had been directly underneath it, he or she could have been killed. No one moves. Everyone stares at the broken pieces, but the guy who plays Gad (one of Joseph's brothers) appears from backstage with a broom and dustpan in hand. The cast begins to disperse while Gad, whose real name is Jeff, sweeps up the broken pieces.

The cast knows only bits and pieces of Jeff's story. He attends another church, but he's part of our cast because the musical director knew him and asked him to audition. His dad died when he was 10, and then his mom died when he was 24. That's when he returned from Europe, where he'd been touring with a singing group, to

become the legal guardian of his 12-year-old sister. He's been raising her now for almost five years. That's about all we know. When
Jeff finishes sweeping the remains of the fallen stage light, the director calls for a full dress rehearsal, so everyone gets in place.

Waiting for my cue, I crouch behind the velvety black theater
curtain while everything backstage becomes a flurry of flying cos-
tumes and props. Then Jeff appears behind me. Dressed as Gad, he
looks as though he just stepped out of the pages of the Bible. As we
listen to the orchestra play the overture, Jeff asks if he can take me
and my daughter to the zoo.

The following Saturday we spend the day trekking all over the
Los Angeles Zoo. The next Saturday we visit the Getty Museum
downtown. The Saturday after that we hike the trails north of Pasadena. These aren't cliché dinner-and-movie kinds of dates. These
are all-day adventures with hours to talk and meals to share. We listen to each other's stories, learning about the events that shaped us.

More than anything, I notice the way Jeff makes me laugh. I'm
not used to laughing. I can't remember having much reason to laugh.
Most of my childhood memories are somber at best. Then young
adulthood turned everything so serious. Every day feels like an extra
layer of gravity pulling on my shoulders, dulling my senses. I don't
know the first thing about how to have a light heart. Until I meet
Jeff.

The truth is, I've never liked people who think they're funny.
Mostly because their humor is the kind of biting sarcasm that comes
at someone else's expense. But Jeff is different. He has a clever way of
finding the levity in irony. He can be fun without being superficial,
serious without being dreary. There's just one problem. Maybe two.
Or two thousand. He's never been married, and I think he deserves
better than me. He's already raised his sister. Who could ask him to
raise another child who isn't his own?

Besides, I'm not sure I want to be married again. In my experience, I'm like Joseph. Things generally don't work out for me. I know Joseph is a rags-to-riches kind of story, but I relate to the rags, not the riches.

I know I can pray anywhere, anytime. But sometimes I feel a strong pull to the altar. I need to pray about whether I should continue this friendship, so I arrange a playdate for my daughter and drive to church. Even though it's a weekday, the doors are open because various small groups are meeting down the hall. The sanctuary, however, sits in stillness. I find a spot on the floor, kneeling at the steps that lead to the stage. I've always felt most at home in God's house.

> Whenever something is weighing on me, this is where I want to be. Alone at the altar.

Whenever something is weighing on me, this is where I want to be. Alone at the altar. My earliest memory is at the altar, playing church in the sanctuary on a weekday while my father/pastor did whatever needed doing. At age 12, I returned often to the altar inside the hospital chapel. At age 17, I was alone at an altar hewn from a fallen tree when I knelt and surrendered my life to Christ.

Now I come and lay every fear on this altar here. I have a litany of reasons why I should run in the opposite direction, why I'd be crazy to entertain the notion of marriage. I hear something stir. A breeze perhaps. Except there isn't a single window in here. I look up and notice the choir loft. I remember the day, three years earlier, when I fainted and fell. Right there on stage. During Sunday morning worship. Unconscious. Broken. I recall the words of Isaiah 54:4-8. I know them by heart.

My eyes move across the stage. It's empty now, but I can envision the way it appeared when our production of *Joseph and the Amazing Technicolor Dreamcoat* transformed it into a dazzling array of color and light. I remember wondering if I should ever dance again. And it was here, on this stage, that dream came true.

> The story of redemption is why we are here.

The velvety black curtain in the back captures my attention. That is where Jeff first asked if he could take me and my daughter to the zoo. And now, a full year later, he's asking me something else. We're talking about the possibility of a future together, and I wonder if all the brokenness of my past could ever be healed. Could anything good ever come from it? Then I remember the most poignant part of Joseph's story, when Joseph said to his brothers,

> You intended to harm me, but God intended it for good
> to accomplish what is now being done, the saving of
> many lives (Genesis 50:20 NIV).

All of Joseph's hardships...The betrayal. The false accusation. The imprisonment. The unfulfilled promise. The wasted years. All of it led to the saving of many lives. What others meant for harm, God meant for good.

The story of Joseph is what brought us together. It's how we met—to be a part of this ancient story of redemption, played out on this very stage. Perhaps it's also why we met. The story of redemption is why we are here.

Jeff calls and tells me he's been meeting with his pastor, a Southern Baptist minister who told him reconciliation is always God's first order. Whenever possible, it's God's heart that marriages are restored. His pastor told him that he needs to talk to my daughter's father, to find out if he has any intention of trying to reconcile. So Jeff asks me for his number, but part of me wants to protest.

"He's been living in another state for a while now. You know that. We hardly see him anymore."

"I know he's not around, but I need to know his intention."

I'm in disbelief. "Are you saying you need his permission to marry me?"

"No, I don't need his permission. I need to know his intention." Jeff remains undeterred.

"Well, okay. I think his intention is pretty clear, but what if he says he wants to reconcile? I can't imagine him saying that. But what if?"

Jeff is slow to respond, then finally says, "Then I need to get out of the picture."

The tone in his voice is steady yet somber. This doesn't sound like something he wants to do, but something he believes he must do because his heart desires to be obedient to God's Word. We both know what the Bible says about divorce and remarriage, and I want to be obedient to God's Word too. I give Jeff the number.

Later that evening Jeff phones me again. "I called him."

"What did he say?"

Jeff says they talked for a few minutes and the response was clear. My former husband has no intention of trying to reconcile.

"Jeff, what did you say when he said that?"

"I told him I'm going to ask you to marry me, and I wanted him to know he would always be welcome in our home whenever he wants to visit his daughter."

"Really? You said that?"

"Of course I did. And I meant it."

I believed him.

> When we yield in obedience to God's voice, He yields a harvest greater than we can imagine.

After 70 years in Babylon all hope was not lost. The record of Ezra's lineage proved him to be a descendant of Hilkiah the high priest.[3] Ezra's great-grandpa, Hilkiah, lived in the day of Israel's disobedience, back when they weren't interested in God's Word. In fact, they'd forgotten all about it and even lost it, but Hilkiah "found the book of the law of the LORD written by the hand of Moses."[4] When he found it, he had it delivered to King Josiah, who wept when they read it to him. King Josiah then initiated major reform throughout Israel. This was Ezra's heritage—a priest who would call God's people back to Him through His Word.

The whole time Ezra was in exile he knew he was called to something more than recordkeeping and scribing in Babylon. He was destined for something far greater, and the day finally came when God arranged for Ezra to return home. Israel's disobedience would no longer keep Ezra in exile. He could go home and resume his heritage as a priest.

This is the mercy of God. Disobedience has consequences, and sometimes they're severe. But when we yield in obedience to God's voice, He yields a harvest greater than we can imagine. Indeed, God redeems "the years the locusts have eaten."[5] He uses our exile as a crucible to teach us and prepare us for something greater. His timetable is not always our timetable. His ways are not always our ways.[6] But the longer we serve God, the more we'll see the way He works on our behalf.

Then a day comes when the shattered pieces of our lives begin to form a mosaic of redemption we couldn't see while we were yet in the middle of so much brokenness. To our own surprise, the sorrow we lived and breathed evaporates, replaced by an unexpected joy. After living in exile, no one is more taken aback when a smile breaks into laughter and we realize it's our own.

14

The Grace We Give

When Jesus had finished [speaking], the crowds were
astonished at His teaching, because He was teaching them
like one who had authority, and not like their scribes.

MATTHEW 7:28-29

I notice Stephanie on the first day of class. She resists every instruction I give. Even the simplest ones. When I ask the class to get out a pen and paper, she's the last to do so. When I ask my students to turn in their papers by passing them to the end of the row where I can pick them up, she's the last to turn hers in. Stephanie is never defiant or disrespectful, but she consistently hesitates to follow instructions. After a few weeks, her resistance to authority seems obvious enough, so I try talking to her after class. I ask her how the semester is going and if there is anything I can do to help, but her answers are curt and uninterested.

As the Thanksgiving holiday nears, I make the same announcement I make every year. Any students who aren't traveling home for Thanksgiving are welcome to come to my house for some turkey, pumpkin pie, and football. Then I scrawl a writing prompt on the board and give the class time to write.

> Sometimes we'll write on paper what we're afraid to speak in person.

These routine writing exercises give me insight into my students' thinking processes as well as their writing abilities. But every once in a while a student turns in a paper that gives a cursory nod at the prompt before launching in another direction. It's not uncommon for students to share deeply personal stories of pain and struggle that have nothing to do with the writing prompt. It's evidence of a heart reaching out. Because sometimes we'll write on paper what we're afraid to speak in person.

I'm sitting on my couch when I read Stephanie's paper, and my then seven-year-old daughter asks, "Mommy, why are you crying?" The writing prompt invited students to share their Thanksgiving traditions and what they're thankful for. Stephanie wrote about her mother, who was diagnosed with schizophrenia and then disappeared when Stephanie was in middle school. She wrote about her father, who abused her, and the many foster homes she stayed in throughout high school. Stephanie's last foster parents helped her fill out an application to this university. She's out of the court system now and on her own. She has no family to go home to for Thanksgiving.

Is it any wonder Stephanie has issues with authority? She's been abandoned and abused by the very people who were supposed to love and protect her.

After our next class meeting, I dismiss the students early and ask Stephanie to stay a few minutes. Once we're alone I thank her for entrusting me with part of her story. Her normal defenses are down. She's able to speak freely now, and we talk about her future.

Meeting Stephanie taught me an important lesson. As teachers, we never know what our students may be going through in their personal lives. The same is true outside the classroom too. We never know what the grouchy cashier might be going through when her shift is over. We never know what the dour person sitting behind us in church may be going through at home either.

I'm pleased when I see a community of college students embracing Stephanie. She comes to class and tells me her roommate has invited her to spend Thanksgiving break at her house. Stephanie's elated.

Twenty years ago I sat where Stephanie sits now. Afraid to tell anyone my story, I showed up for class and pretended to be normal like everyone else. When I signed up for a required biblical studies class on 1 and 2 Samuel, I assumed I already knew everything about those books because they were two of my favorites in the Bible.

When the professor asks us to name David's gravest sin, the other students seem as confident as I am in basic Bible knowledge. How about lust? Adultery? Murder? King David took another man's wife, got her pregnant, and then had her husband killed in battle. What could be worse than murder?

> God makes it clear we'll be held accountable for what we know and what we've been given.

The professor shakes his head at our obvious answers and reminds us that all sin separates us from God. Sins are not ranked in terms of bad to worse. The severity of a sin's offense lies in the damage it causes and the consequences it incurs. Then he leans on the desk at the front of the room and says, "King David's most serious sin was his abuse of power."

I admit I wasn't expecting that one, but the more I listen and the more I contemplate what I know to be true of God's Word, it makes sense. Throughout the Bible God makes it clear we'll be held accountable for what we know and what we've been given. To whom much is given, much is required.[1]

King David was given a lot. Riches. Fame. Power. All of it was his, but he grew complacent. When he was supposed to be in battle with his soldiers, he stayed behind in the luxury of his palace. And when he encountered temptation, he wanted what he wanted when he wanted it. This time what he wanted was her—Uriah's wife, Bathsheba. Since David was king, no one would deny him, so he abused his power to take whatever—and whomever—he wanted. And he got rid of anyone in his way. King David's abuse of power was his most serious offense.

For Thanksgiving we make the trip up north and spend an evening around the table with family, telling stories and eating pie. Somehow the topic turns to speeding tickets and the number of times we've been pulled over. When it's Kendall's turn, he says,

> I'm driving home late one night and I have a can of Coke between my legs. As I turn a corner, the can flips over and my car swerves as I reach for it. Well, sure enough, a cop pulls me over, assuming I'm a drunk driver. Except I haven't had anything to drink.
>
> I pull over and roll down my window and give the officer my driver's license and registration. Then he asks me to step out of my car. So I say, "Sure thing, but I need to reach in the back and get my wheelch…" The officer cuts me off and barks for me to get out of the car.
>
> I open my door and tell the officer I'm going to reach in the back, and he yells at me to put my hands on the

steering wheel. I do as he says, but then I can only sit there. The officer is getting mad at me for not getting out of my car, but every time I try to talk, he yells at me to shut up and get out of the car. I try to explain to him, but he won't listen. He just assumes I'm being insubordinate.

Then he grabs my jacket by the shoulders and pulls me out of the car, thinking I'll stand up. But when he lets go, I fall to the ground. Then he says, "Oh, you're so drunk you can't even stand up, huh?" Well, now I'm really mad and I start yelling at the cop, telling him I'm paralyzed and that I was trying to tell him I needed my wheelchair but he wouldn't let me talk.

When he looks inside my car and sees my hand controls and my wheelchair in the back, I can see the blood draining from his face as he realizes I'm telling the truth. So there I am, lying on the ground, and he just backs away. He gets in his police car and drives off, leaving me on the pavement. I had to drag myself back to my car with my arms and pull myself inside.

I'm so horrified I don't even have words. I want blood. I want vengeance. For a fleeting moment my only consolation is a sincere hope that God has a special place in hell for someone like that. Then I remember what my professor once said—that God hates it whenever someone abuses their power.

> God wants us to know we can go to Him with everything— even the really ugly.

The Hebrews experienced the most horrific abuse of power imaginable when the Babylonians invaded Jerusalem. Their power was brute strength, and it's not surprising that some Hebrews harbored a deep hatred toward their enemies. In Psalm 137 we're allowed a brief glimpse into the thoughts of one exile:

> Daughter Babylon, doomed to destruction, happy is the one who pays you back what you have done to us. Happy is he who takes your little ones and dashes them against the rocks (Psalm 137:8-9).

What in the world? Who could possibly wish harm on someone's children? What kind of pain must this exile have endured to want such a vile revenge?

The words of this psalm are severe—so severe, in fact, I've yet to hear a Sunday sermon on them. What do you do with that? And yet the Bible refuses to gloss over the hard and the ugly. The Bible records the human condition with alarming accuracy, because God wants us to know we can go to Him with everything—even the really ugly.[2]

As I lie in bed that night, I soak my pillow with seething anger. What kind of person would drag a paraplegic out of his car and then leave him on the ground and drive away? And this wasn't just any person. This was a police officer! Someone who swore an oath to serve and protect!

King David had also sworn an oath to serve and protect, but there was a season in his life when he failed miserably. He abused his power. What's notable, though, is not his crime but his confession. When the prophet Nathan confronted him, King David confessed and repented. With genuine remorse he went to God in prayer.

> God, create a clean heart for me and renew a steadfast spirit within me...Save me from the guilt of bloodshed (Psalm 51:10,14).

A new future with a new hope awaits.

His sin was serious, but so was his confession. That's the difference. When we take our ugliest junk to God, He removes our sin from us as far as the east is from the west.[3]

The first thing I learned in my class on 1 and 2 Samuel was how seriously God feels about any abuse of power. The second thing I learned was that 1 and 2 Chronicles, which basically rehash all the stories told in 1 and 2 Samuel and 1 and 2 Kings, omit King David's failure. History wasn't rewritten; it wasn't changed to say David's sin never happened. But the chronicler left it out, in all likelihood to remind the returning exiles of God's complete forgiveness. Their past sins will not be held against them. A new future with a new hope awaits.

The chronicler is the anonymous person credited for writing 1 and 2 Chronicles and arranging the psalms in the order we have today. The chronicler was obviously someone who lived in the post-exilic period of Israel—the most likely candidate being Ezra because his own book begins at the same place 2 Chronicles ends.

We know Ezra organized the scribes and passed on the heritage of preserving God's Word. Those scribes fulfilled an important purpose, as the ancient scrolls we have today authenticate the canon of Holy Scripture. But even the scribes, the ones who knew Scripture best, eventually veered from God's path.

> No one could hear Jesus preach and not hear the gospel of grace.

Within a few generations, the scribes became know-it-alls who lorded their knowledge over people. They added oral tradition to God's written law and imposed an impossible standard on everyone. By the time Jesus was born, the scribes were verifiable Pharisees with an ugly self-righteousness to match.

When Jesus taught Scripture, the people were amazed because He spoke with authority—the kind of authority that genuinely cares for people and never lords knowledge or power over others. No one could hear Jesus preach and not hear the gospel of grace. Such grace seemed scandalous to His listeners, but centuries earlier the chronicler foreshadowed this grace when he omitted David's failure from the history books.

It's the message of hope we all have. If we've asked God for forgiveness, our sins won't be counted against us. They're blotted from the records. Just as David's failure with Bathsheba and Uriah is not mentioned in 1 and 2 Chronicles, our failures are never mentioned again—not by God.

The same grace available for King David is available for me, for you, and even the police officer who treated my brother so horribly. God's grace is available for all.

The story of the great flood is one of the most frequently told stories to children, especially in Sunday school. We show cartoon pictures of animals walking two by two into the ark, and they typically depict a sunny sky behind tame zebras and lions. The entire scene glows with serenity. Until the rain begins. But don't worry. Everyone is safe and warm inside the ark, and pretty soon a giant rainbow will grace a new, blue sky. The end.

I've taught this story to toddlers and preschoolers countless times. After all, Noah obeyed God even when "water falling from the sky" had never happened before and didn't make any sense. Obedience is like that sometimes. It requires a faith that doesn't always make sense. Noah trusted and obeyed, and God protected him and his family.

When I read the biblical account of the flood, however, and not a children's version of it, I see a different picture. I still see faithful Noah and an ark filled with animals, but I also see the multitudes who died. They disobeyed God, time and again, until time ran out.

The real story of the flood is gruesome. Water covered the earth. As did death.

For some reason, I always remember that it rained for 40 days and 40 nights, but I forget it took a year for the water to recede. Anyone who has ever experienced a serious flood knows the rains may last a few days, but it can take months and sometimes years to recover from flood damage. The same is true with any metaphorical storm. A drowned dream. A flooded friendship. A submerged marriage. Life after a flood can take a long time to heal. But healing does come.

When Noah and his family were finally able to leave the ark and release the animals, God did indeed bless them. Then He commanded them to "be fruitful and multiply."[4] Here again we see an echo of Christ's salvation to come. With Noah, salvation was physical. God spared their lives when He judged the people of earth. With Jesus, salvation is spiritual. Jesus came to save us from spiritual death, to offer eternal life to all who believe. And to those who accept Christ's free gift, He gives this command:

> With Noah, salvation was physical. With Jesus, salvation is spiritual.

> Go...and make disciples of all nations, baptizing them in the name of the Father and of the Son and of the Holy Spirit (Matthew 28:19).

In the Old Testament, God commanded Noah and his family to be fruitful and multiply in a physical sense. In the New Testament,

God commands believers who have been saved by grace to be fruitful and multiply in a spiritual sense—by making disciples.

This is God's command for all believers. To live a life of obedience to God is to make disciples, and that's what Part Four of this
book is about.

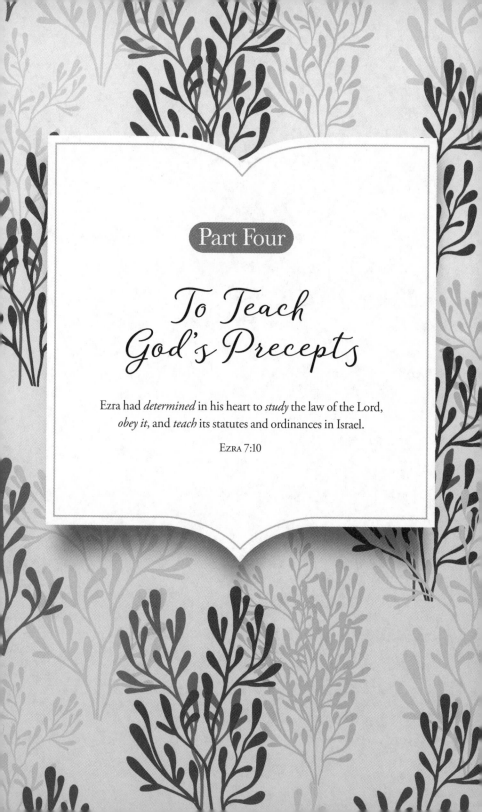

Part Four

To Teach God's Precepts

Ezra had *determined* in his heart to *study* the law of the Lord, *obey it*, and *teach* its statutes and ordinances in Israel.

Ezra 7:10

15

The Women We Welcome

*Encourage one another and build each
other up as you are already doing.*

1 Thessalonians 5:11

I sit at my computer desk with a hot cup of tea, ready to work on a to-do list a mile long. The house is quiet, but through an open window I hear a bird chirping, and in the distance I hear the school bell ring. We live a couple of blocks from my daughter's school, so when I hear the bell I imagine my 12-year-old daughter walking to class with her friends.

After finishing my tea, I dive into my first work project for the day. When I hear sirens rushing past, I pause to say a quick prayer, like I always do, for whomever the ambulance is racing to help. Moments later my phone rings and I recognize the school's number. I register the sirens again and grab my phone.

The voice on the other end says, "Mrs. Hughes, I work at your daughter's school. She swallowed something and began choking..."

Before the lady can finish her sentence I'm halfway out the door. "Your daughter couldn't breathe...She collapsed on the ground..." I'm in my car, listening to this lady talk while also praying. Praying hard. "I'm told your daughter has regained consciousness but...she's in an ambulance now...can you come straight to the school?"

I'm already there.

I park my car at an awkward angle behind the ambulance and run past the principal. My Brynn is strapped to a gurney with a mask over her face. The paramedic tells me the percentage of her oxygenation, and he says something else, but all I hear is, "She's going to be okay." He says they need to take her to the hospital for evaluation, but I'm still focused on the part where he said she's going to be okay. I rub Brynn's leg because it's the only part of her I can reach, and I tell her I'm here.

An ambulance ride later we're in the emergency room, answering questions and filling out forms. As Brynn answers the doctor's questions, I hear the whole story. A friend passed around chocolate Easter eggs. When Brynn popped one in her mouth, it got stuck in her throat and she couldn't breathe. No air was getting through. None. To get her friends' attention, she waved her arms and pointed to her throat.

> We need girlfriends who reach for our hand when we can't breathe.

One friend (whose dad is a police officer with LAPD) immediately called 9-1-1 on her cell phone, quickly explained the situation, and gave the school's street address. Another friend who happens to be the fastest runner in the seventh grade (her parents are track and field coaches) took off running toward the school office to find an adult. Another friend, who had just taken a first aid class to become a babysitter, tried to do the Heimlich. And another friend held her hand and cried.

Her friends reported that Brynn's lips turned blue and she fell to the ground unconscious. About that time they could hear the sirens coming. And two blocks away a mom offered up a prayer for "whomever" needed help.

While sitting in the ER, I marvel at the way her friends responded. They're only 12 years old, but they didn't panic. They didn't freeze.

Each of them reacted with quick thinking, and I couldn't be more grateful. We all need girlfriends who rush to our sides when we most need help. We need girlfriends who respond to situations with wisdom and care. We need girlfriends who reach for our hands when we can't breathe.

We need each other. When a child is ill. When bills loom large. When depression creeps in. When a marriage falls apart. We need friends who are there *for* us and will pray *with* us. That's the kind of friend I want to be.

> We need friends who are there *for* us and will pray *with* us.

I must confess, however, that I've always felt a little handicapped when it comes to the whole girlfriend thing. One, I never had sisters, so I didn't have much opportunity to practice girlfriend talk while growing up. Two, I'm more introverted by nature, so when I'm with a group of girlfriends, I tend to be one of the quieter ones. I enjoy listening, but I don't always have something to say. Nevertheless, I know it's important for women to gather. Even when we're from different family backgrounds and have different past experiences, something beautiful can happen when women are together.

The book of Philippians is my favorite example. We're told in Acts 16 that the apostle Paul was traveling through Asia when he had a dream. Basically, God told him in a dream not to go any further into Asia. Instead, Paul should go to Macedonia, which we call Greece. So Paul and his companions traveled to Greece and entered the city of Philippi.

Philippi didn't have a synagogue, but Paul heard about a group of women that gathered by the river on the Sabbath to pray. So he went to the river and preached the cross of Christ. That day a woman named Lydia and her whole household determined in their hearts to follow Jesus. Paul baptized them right there in the river.

And the first church in Europe was born. That's what can happen when women gather.

Years later Paul was imprisoned in Rome and wrote a letter to his friends back in Philippi. That letter would later be inducted into the canon of Holy Scripture as the book we call Philippians. The book of Philippians is the subsequent fruit born of a few women. That's what can happen when women gather.

> We learn best when we learn from each other.

Gathering is important. Scripture says we should not neglect the habit of meeting together.[1] We should "encourage one another and build each other up."[2] Still, we've probably all experienced what can happen when women gather, yet they don't encourage one another or build each other up. In those situations we can't get away fast enough.

I've been to a lot of women's gatherings. From baby showers to playdates. From bunko parties to girls' nights out. I have fun memories from many different get-togethers, but my favorite time with other women is when we gather to study God's Word. Women can minister to other women in unique ways. We need each other's wisdom and counsel and guidance. We need each other's stories and laughter and tears. Because we learn best when we learn from each other.

I moved a lot in my early twenties, so I didn't have much opportunity for a group of girlfriends in my life, much less a mentor. I often wished I had someone who could watch me grow into adulthood as a wife and mom. Someone who could encourage me and challenge me as a child of God. But I was always the new girl at church. My Bible and my books were my constant companions—sometimes my only companions.

One day I made a list of my favorite authors who had significantly influenced the way I think and live. To my dismay, I realized they all had something in common: They were all men. They were great men, no doubt, and I noticed they were mostly pastors and a few professors, like C.S. Lewis. But my list had a glaring omission. Where were the women? How could I grow to become the woman God wanted me to be without women to help show me the way?

My list prompted me to do two things. I joined the women's prayer group at church and I went to the Christian bookstore looking for female authors. You already know how the prayer meetings turned out, but at the Christian bookstore I found a women's devotional Bible. It had writings interspersed throughout the biblical text. The women on these pages—their voices and their stories—became a lifeline for me during a long stretch of years when I didn't have older women in my life. By reading their stories and hearing how Scripture made an impact on them, I caught a glimpse of what Christian womanhood could look like.

This was before the days of the Internet, so it wasn't like it is today when you can swipe your smartphone and look up someone's website. These women's stories were printed and bound between the covers of my Bible, and I carried them with me to church. They opened my eyes to the women around me too. Instead of looking for someone my age to connect with, I looked for women who might resemble the ones I was reading about.

I began watching the older women at church. To be sure, there were some I didn't want to emulate, but there were others with an easy demeanor. A quiet confidence. A sure smile. A soft word. During the meet-and-greet time on Sunday morning, the portion of the service I normally dreaded, I approached the women I admired. Over time I got to know some of them. Just as women gathered by the river with Lydia in Acts 16, I gathered with women who inspired me at church. They were my first Lydias.

C.S. Lewis was part of a writers' group that met regularly to critique each other's work. They called themselves the Inklings. This little band of English creatives—including writers such as J.R.R. Tolkien and Owen Barfield—created a space where they could spur one another in their gifting. Their group is a beautiful example of how an individual can benefit by being around others who share a similar passion and purpose.

We'll never grow deep friendships with women if we can't learn to truly love those who are different from us.

I dreamed of doing something like that with women, but I made two critical errors. First, I prayed for God to send me a mentor. I wanted a godly woman who loved Scripture and could explain the more confusing parts of the Bible to me. I wanted someone who would listen to me share about my life, my struggles, and my dreams. I wanted someone who would give me sage advice when I needed to make an important decision. And if possible, I wanted someone who could teach me how to make a casserole for the next church potluck, preferably without burning it.

God never answered this prayer. He never sent me a one-size-fits-all mentor. Instead He brought multiple women into my life. One who loved to study Scripture. Another who loved to steep tea and savor long conversations. Still another who was skilled in making casseroles. And He brought many, many more.

The second mistake I made was that I kept looking for people just like me. I wanted to find a "kindred spirit"—several of them, in fact—so we could form our own little group of Inklings. But every person I tried to get to know turned out to be different from me. I'm pretty sure God planned it that way. We'll never grow deep, long-lasting friendships with women if we can't learn to truly love those who are different from us.

One time I met a writer named September, and I was too quick to assume we had nothing in common. She lives in upstate New York, has ten kids, and homeschools all of them all the way through high school. As soon as I learned this I thought, *She lives on the East Coast. I live on the West Coast. She has ten kids. I have three kids. She homeschools her kids. My kids attend public school. We couldn't possibly have anything in common.*

But I couldn't have been more wrong. As I listened to her story, I heard a woman who shares the same passion for Jesus I have. I heard a woman who is full of compassion for others, who opens her home and invites women in.

> We see this throughout the Bible—not stories of similar people, but stories of different people who came together for a common purpose.

God taught me an important lesson. I had made an assumption based on external circumstances, but when I took the time to listen, I realized September and I had so much more in common than I first imagined. Ever since that day she has become one of my dearest friends.

We see this throughout the Bible—not stories of similar people, but stories of different people who came together for a common purpose. The whole Jerusalem project—rebuilding the city and the temple—required multiple leaders who spanned decades. Zerubbabel led the first caravan home, and his primary task was to oversee the reconstruction of the temple. Ezra led the second caravan home, and his main focus was to teach the Word of God and restore the temple rituals and sacrifices. Nehemiah led the third caravan home, and his chief concern was rebuilding the walls around the city. The reconstruction of Jerusalem didn't happen because of one person or one leader. It took many. Each person was called by God to accomplish a different task, and they were obedient to the call God had placed on their lives.

We can follow their example today. We can work together to create spaces of welcome where women from different backgrounds can gather to study God's Word. We need safe places where we can grow closer to God and to each other—in our homes and in our churches. Many Bible studies are already taking place in virtually every town and city across North America, but it's up to us to determine what kind of gathering a newcomer will find. Will they find women who encourage one another and build each other up?

We know Ezra determined in his heart to study the law of the Lord and obey it, but he didn't stop there. He also taught God's Word. Not everyone is called to be a teacher in the strictest sense of the word, but everyone has a part to play in God's kingdom. Maybe you don't feel called to teach the Bible, but you might know how to make a casserole or gluten-free bread. Chances are someone at your church would really like to meet you. Maybe you don't feel qualified to mentor someone, but you do love coffee and conversation. I'd bet there's a woman in your community who is praying to meet someone just like you.

> We don't need an official title or position to be women who reach out and minister to other women.

We can be women who gather to study God's Word, to encourage one another, and to build each other up. Maybe a woman sitting next to you at Bible study is going through something similar you once went through. Perhaps God has placed you there so you can encourage that sister in Christ. I'll never forget the women who have been an encouragement to me.

- I don't know the nurse's name who put her hand on my 12-year-old shoulder and gave me a can of Sprite, but I'll always remember her kindness.
- I'll always remember the way Juanita held me the morning I fainted in choir and told her what was really happening in my life.
- I'll always be grateful for the single moms at the preschool where I worked. Because of their willingness to watch my daughter a couple evenings a week, I could continue taking college classes at night.

Through their examples and many more, I've learned to keep my eyes open to notice those hurting around me.

We don't need an official title or position to be women who reach out and minister to other women. When Jesus met the woman at the well, a woman with a painful past and a not-so-glamorous present, He offered her living water. A fresh start. A second chance. And she was never the same. She ran to share the grace and truth of Jesus Christ with everyone she knew. Then more lives were changed.[3] The Samaritan woman didn't have to go to seminary or join a church staff or start a blog to

> When women walk through the doors of our homes and churches, we want every heart to know they're welcome.

become a voice of hope in her community. She simply shared Jesus with others.

We can do this today. When women walk through the doors of our homes and churches, we want every heart to know they're welcome—that nothing in their past can bar them from God's love. God's forgiveness is complete. The reason we're here is because of the grace we've been given through the sacrifice Jesus made on the cross.

We can be like my daughter's friends, who each did the one thing they knew how to do. And if we feel like we don't have the skill needed for a particular occasion, that's okay too. Sometimes the most important thing we can do is hold a friend's hand when she can't breathe. When a woman is still bleeding from a miscarriage. When her husband has just lost his job. When her adult child isn't walking with the Lord. When her husband tells her he's leaving...and there's someone else. We can be there. Sharing the tears and holding her hand. Because we're women of the Word—women of grace and women of truth.

16

The Roots We Plant

Blessed is the one...whose delight is in the law of the LORD,
and who meditates on his law day and night.
That person is like a tree planted by streams of water,
which yields its fruit in season and whose leaf does not wither
—whatever they do prospers.

PSALM 1:1-3 NIV

The wind screeched with a deafening cry as it rushed about in speeds uncommon. Having grown up in California, I wasn't used to this kind of weather. The most the wind had ever accomplished around these parts was the mere rustle of a few leaves or the slight tussle of a few bangs. But this wind blew with fury.

I could do little else but sit and listen and watch the local news. The weatherman called it a once-in-a-century windstorm. I thought storms included rain and hail, thunder and lightning. I'd even heard of dust storms. But a windstorm? That was new to this California native, and I can tell you I didn't like the sound of it. Something fierce was happening outside, and I was glad not to be in it.

I clung to the bedcovers a little tighter that night, and prayed a little longer. By morning the wind had traveled south and an eerie silence followed in its place. I brushed the window curtain aside to see a mess of palm branches and tree limbs strewn about the yard. Up and down the street trash cans were tipped over, spilling out.

Flower beds lay flattened. Across the cul-de-sac an old ash tree lay horizontal, its bare limbs pointing awkwardly straight toward the sky. At the base of the tree a tangle of roots revealed what was once hidden. The roots hadn't been deep enough to withstand the power of the storm. The tree's anchor had given way.

When I think about the potential we have today to minister to women in our community as well as online, I remember that tree.

I zipped my suitcase tight with everything I needed for the weekend but forgot one thing. I looked at Jeff and confessed, "I can't remember why I signed up for this." Why was I flying across the country to spend several days with Christian women? Hadn't I learned my lesson?

> Some of my favorite memories are with women circled around God's Word—studying, learning, and growing together.

Through a friend online I heard about this conference for women who want to share Christ with other women through teaching and writing. I love teaching and I love writing. But women? I'd rather stay home. Some of my favorite memories are with women circled around God's Word—studying, learning, and growing together. Some of my most painful memories, however, also involve circles of women. We're a funny breed. With great potential in either direction.

Standing at the airport's curb, I wanted to climb back into our minivan, drive home, and forget this crazy notion of flying thousands of miles to meet women I didn't even know. Blogging was easier. It provided a safe distance. I could write about Bible verses easily enough, but I wouldn't write about the turmoil in my soul. I wouldn't write about the pain that drove me away from ministry.

But then, while holding my suitcase on the airport curb with taxis whizzing past us, I remembered why I signed up to attend.

I'd withdrawn from the church I'd been serving in for almost a decade. My small group had splintered and left everyone bleeding or nursing a grudge. What started as a misunderstanding grew into gossip and later into a full-fledged war between two women. The rest of us either took a side or stepped out of it altogether. I stepped out when it was clear some members of the group were not interested in forgiveness and reconciliation.

I preferred the company of bloggers after that. Bloggers are tiny thumbnail pictures with people on the other side of a screen. If anything happens to get crossways, you can turn off your computer and go about your day. But God's voice continued to penetrate my heart: *Trust Me. Love others.* So with a prayer and a plane ticket, I flew across the country to meet some women in person. To bridge the distance between our computers.

For three days I listened to speakers and observed women doing life and ministry together, both on stage and off. I witnessed women in ministry—not women in misery. They weren't in competition with each other; rather, they were serving one another. They were *for* each other.

> I witnessed women in ministry—not women in misery.

I met women who loved God and wanted to be a vessel of grace in His kingdom. We stayed up half the night talking, laughing, and crying. As I listened to their stories and their dreams, I realized we shared a passion for God and His Word. I also realized how God was using the global church to heal some of the wounds I experienced in my local church. My heart began to heal that weekend as

God restored my love for women and my deep desire to see them transformed by His Word. I flew home with a heart full and a mind swimming with possibilities.

> I want to build bridges in the kingdom. Bridges between women. And bridges between churches.

Yes, bad experiences between women can, and likely will, happen. When it's bad, it's really bad. But when it's good, it's really good. And what I want more than anything is for women to come together and experience the good that can come from women ministering to women. I want to build bridges in the kingdom. Bridges between women. And bridges between churches. Because God has already created the greatest Bridge of all, through His Son, Jesus, to bridge the gap between God and us.

About this time I invited some "online friends" to join me in reading the chronological Bible. The Bible we read from had 365 readings, and each day we read the selected passage and then met on a private Facebook page to discuss the reading. I loved hearing their insights into Scripture. We became Team 365—women reading God's Word every day. Eventually I started a website, and we took turns sharing our insights from the daily reading, inviting everyone to join the discussion in the comments. Team 365 included women from every region in North America, including Canada. Eventually, more women around the globe joined us for the daily readings and discussions.

I found myself investing in women more and more in an online ministry context, which wasn't a bad thing at all. But the more time I spent at my computer, the less time I wanted to spend with women at church. Frankly, the women on the other side of my computer still seemed nicer, safer. I didn't want to admit it, but I was hiding again, choosing to be invisible in my own community. So I asked

God to show me what I should do. Should I log off forever? Or keep going like it's no big deal?

When I prayed, the picture of that fallen ash tree on our street came to mind, and I knew what it meant. The leafy, visible portion of the tree is our online life and the root system is our local life. The height and health of our online reach will mirror the depth we're connected to our local community and invested in our local church.

I knew what God was asking me to do. He wasn't saying I needed to give up my online ministry to women, but He was telling me I needed to be sure my roots were planted deep in my local community and church. That meant showing up. To things like Bible study. The kind where you sit in a room, face-to-face with other women. I'd always enjoyed this before, but the hurts made me want to disappear.

The solace I found in online communities and at conferences was a time for healing, and they continue to be sources of enjoyment. But the image of that tree has become my analogy for ministry—to be globally minded while also locally grounded.

Not everyone will feel the call to a "global" kind of ministry. And that's okay. But every believer is called to be an ambassador for Christ wherever they call home.[1] This is why it's so important for us as believers to be rooted in the community we live in, serving our families and neighborhoods and local churches.

> We need to be globally minded and locally grounded.

One Saturday we armed our kids with disposable cameras and visited Descanso Gardens near Pasadena. They have a little train ride you can take as a family, and then you walk through a rose garden, a Japanese garden, and the largest camellia collection on the continent. The kids snapped away with their cameras while I took pictures with my phone.

One section is called the Oak Forest and for good reason. Massive oaks stand next to each other, their foliage so thick the sun can't reach the earth. A stroll through the shady Oak Forest reminds you of those movies about the Middle Ages in Europe, where the men ride stallions with swords on their belts and the women wear long dresses and hats the shape of tall cones, with gauzy scarves flowing out the top. The landscape is so picturesque that professional photographers take turns standing at certain vista points to take pictures. The writer in me wanted to script a scene, but the only words that came to mind were Isaiah's: "They will be called oaks of righteousness, a planting of the LORD for the display of his splendor" (61:3 NIV).

> When we plant our roots deep, nourished by the living water of the Word, we become a glorious display of the Lord's splendor.

I always thought it was strange of Isaiah to liken God's people to oak trees. People are living, breathing, fleshly creatures. Not branches and leaves. But walking through the Oak Forest changed my perspective. I imagined the roots beneath my feet, deep underground. These oaks are more than a hundred years old. Their roots are likely mingled together, making them even stronger. Then I thought about the windstorm that had swept through Southern California with unprecedented force. Unlike the ash tree on my street, these oaks were still standing, and they were standing together.

That's the picture Isaiah gave. God's people, standing strong and standing together. Isaiah was prophesying about the exiles who would return to Jerusalem someday to rebuild the temple and the city. There would be hard times with obstacles to overcome. But if they stayed together, in community, and planted their roots deep, where the living water of the Word could nourish their souls, they would become a glorious display of the Lord's splendor.

Isaiah's promise to the exiles is a promise for us today. Like Ezra, we can determine in our hearts to study God's Word and obey His voice. These are all great things—necessary even. But God never intended for us to do them alone. Just as Ezra brought people together to read God's Word to them, we can gather with women to study God's Word and learn how to discern His voice.

Together we can become oaks of righteousness.

The Story We Share

Older women are...to teach what is good,
so they may encourage the young women.

TITUS 2:3-4

Years ago I met two midwives who became a dear part of our family's story. For nine months they walked alongside me. They encouraged me. And when the time came, they came too. Their quiet demeanor graced the room as they moved softly about, there but not there. They checked on me every so often, but mostly they created an atmosphere where my husband and I could labor together, bringing new life into the world.

Their presence was a gift to me. They possessed an intuitive sense of when to let nature be and when to step in if I needed care. For a long time afterward I fancied the idea of doing the same for other women. To be there. To encourage and support. To bear witness to the beauty of new life.

> Dreams are sometimes birthed one way and realized another way.

I turned my thoughts into action and researched the years of study required, first to become a nurse, then a certified nurse-midwife. With my plan in place, I spoke my dream. I waited until our tiny cherub slept, and then told my husband how I'd like to become a midwife.

Jeff nodded as he listened. When I finished, I waited for his response, but his words were slow in coming. Finally he said, "Denise, I think you'd be a great midwife. I can understand why you're drawn to the idea. But I think after a while you'd miss teaching and writing."

Even as he spoke I knew he was right. I was created to work with words and shape ideas. To break the waters on the page and bring forth new life in a different way. Yet something inside me still longed to come alongside women—in a quiet, soft, encouraging way.

I never could have imagined how dreams are sometimes birthed one way and realized another way.

A woman I recently met at church sends me an email, asking if we can get together. When I meet Kay for lunch, I come prepared to listen. To hear her story. To hear her heart. Her children are grown; one is in college and the other is married. Now that she's officially an empty nester, she's been praying about this next season in her life. She wants to come alongside young women, especially mothers with small children. Because she's been there. She gets it. But she's not sure where to begin or if young women would be interested in what she wants to share.

She's afraid.

I see a kind woman in her middle years who wants to serve other women. I also see passion mixed with hesitation, desire mingled with fear. After 45 minutes, Kay leans in close and lowers her voice, as if to make a confession of the direst sorts. "I have this idea. It's really just a list. I've written down some things I want to share with young moms. I think it would help them. These things really helped me when my kids were little, and I want to pass them on. I want to speak. Is that crazy? I mean, I know I'm not a speaker. Not like our pastor on Sunday mornings. And I know I can't speak like the ladies on the DVDs at our mid-week Bible study. But there's something inside me, and I can't shake it. I think I'd really like to do it. I'd like to try."

She stops abruptly and leans against the back of her chair, turning her face aside, pushing back tears. "I'm in a small group with several women," she says. "We're all about the same age, and we've been meeting for a couple of years now. I was afraid to tell them

> Where *does* a woman go if she has the desire to teach other women?

what I've been feeling, but one night I decided to be brave. We were talking about our dreams, so I told them about mine. That I want to speak to young women about motherhood."

Her shoulders drop as she looks into her lap. "They were shocked. Two friends said I should go for it. What have I got to lose? The rest just nodded half-heartedly. I could tell they didn't think I could do it, but one of them actually said so. She said I wasn't qualified to speak on motherhood because I don't have a degree in counseling or child development or something like that. She said I couldn't do it."

She said I couldn't do it. That's what my friend heard, so she thought she shouldn't even try.

I'm afraid she's not alone. I've talked with many women like Kay who wonder the same thing. *Can I teach? Would other women be interested in listening? Is it too late for me? Would women my own age be supportive of me? How would I even begin something like that? Could I really do it? Would I run out of things to say? Could I keep an audience tuned in for more than five minutes? What if I'm not any good?*

So many questions. So many doubts. With so few places to turn. So few people to ask. Where *does* a woman go if she has the desire to teach other women?

When we think of teaching, we think of the classroom and credentials. I love the classroom, but when I look over the four-plus decades of my life, the women who influenced me the most weren't teachers in a classroom. They were women in pews on Sunday morning, women at Bible study on Tuesday night, and women in my living room on Saturday afternoon. The most influential women in my life are the ones who have touched my life in some way. The ones who have connected with me personally.

There's something sacred about gathering in person, where live voices are heard and hands are held and hearts are touched.

I'm committed to the women's weekly Bible study at my church. It's one of the ways I'm intentional about planting roots in my local church. Every Tuesday night the sanctuary is filled with round tables, women gathered around each one. I sit at a table with seven other women, and I've written their names in my prayer journal so I can pray for them during the week. I ask God to show me how I might encourage each one the next time we meet.

I'm not the "teacher." We don't have one. We do what a lot of churches do—we buy studies that come with DVDs. We do our homework during the week and then gather to listen to the teacher on the screen. I've been a part of these kinds of Bible studies for over 15 years, and I've learned some wonderful things. But the most meaningful time is when we turn our chairs toward each other and listen to each woman's story. We listen to her tell about her experience as she read the Bible that week. We listen to what the Holy Spirit is saying to her in a specific situation. We listen, we encourage, and, when appropriate, we offer guidance.

There's something sacred about gathering in person, where live voices are heard and hands are held and hearts are touched. Something special happens when souls wrapped in flesh come together to learn about God and each other. Jesus said as much when He stated, "For where two or three are gathered together in My name, I am there among them."[1]

One year the women at church inquired about a women's retreat, a weekend away. They used to have annual retreats, but then they stopped. So I asked our pastor's wife why. She said it was too much work and too many feelings got hurt.

"What happened?"

"The last time we went on a weekend retreat," she said, "the woman in charge of hospitality got mad that no one was helping her in the kitchen. She felt like she was doing all the work while everyone else got to sit around and drink coffee and visit. She wanted to visit too. There were maybe 25 of us. We had rented a big house in the mountains, but the women stayed in smaller groups the whole time. These three here wanted to stay together. Those four there wanted to stay together. It was hard to get everybody together for a large group

> When women create memories together, away from their normal day-to-day activities, friendships deepen.

session. Basically, it was a whole lot of work and some people felt left out, so we stopped having weekend retreats. It wasn't worth it."

Her story made me sad. When women create memories together, away from their normal day-to-day activities, friendships deepen. A group of us at church wanted to make a retreat happen again, so we got the green light from the church leadership and started planning. We found a retreat center that provided a kitchen staff and a room for us to meet in. The lodging was simplistic; we'd need to bring our own bed linens, but we were fine with that.

Our next hurdle was finding a speaker. We were pretty sure our favorite DVD speakers wouldn't be available to speak at a weekend retreat for maybe 40 or 50 women. But then, who else was there? We didn't know any speakers personally. Then one woman in our group sat straight up and said, "Hey. What if, I mean, this might sound weird, but we have four sessions, right? Friday night, Saturday morning, Saturday night, and Sunday morning. What if we asked four women from our church to speak? One for each session? Each woman could share her story of how she met Jesus and how He's transformed her life."

Her idea was met with silence as we tried to imagine what that might look like. Finally another woman broke the silence and said, "Like who? Who would we ask?"

A few names were shared as possibilities, and we agreed to pray about it. At our next planning meeting, the decision was unanimous—four different women from our own congregation would speak. And they wanted me to be one of them.

Months later we piled into minivans and caravanned to the retreat center. We were a little nervous. But we'd prayed and planned and prayed some more, and we trusted God would meet us and move however He desired. We had a theme and a schedule with four main sessions, but we also included some free time so the women could relax and get to know each other better.

At each session we sang a few worship choruses and then listened to one woman from our church share her story. We cried every time. There were whole chapters in their lives we knew nothing about. On Sunday morning it was my turn. I talked about the long arm of the Lord. No matter how dark things get, no matter how far from God we feel, we're never beyond His reach. I shared parts of my story most of the women in the room had never heard.

Something transpired at this retreat. Every time a woman shared her story, other women shared theirs. Late at night, sitting on bunk beds. Early in the morning, eating in the cafeteria. Women opened up and shared. I'd been attending this church for several years. Jeff and I were both serving in leadership and actively involved in ministry. Yet there were chapters of my life I'd never had the opportunity to share. The invitation to share my story opened doors to more conversations with women who wanted to talk afterward.

> Women need other women to open up and share their lives.

I can't count how many women's retreats I've been to over the years, but this one retreat changed the way I viewed women's ministry and the Titus 2 mandate for older women to teach younger women. Women need other women to open up and share their lives—how they met Jesus, how they spend time in the Word, how they pray, how they manage work life and home life. If they're married, how they love their husbands. If they're moms, how they survived the toddler years and teen years. What women need is an invitation to share.

When it was time to plan the next Bible study, we did something a little different. We still bought a 10-week study that came with DVDs, but we planned to complete that 10-week study in 20 weeks. We slowed the pace to give everyone more time to finish each session's homework, and every other week, when we didn't show a DVD, we asked a woman in our congregation to share instead. It was our way of getting "the best of both worlds." It worked for us.

That summer we took another plunge. We selected several parables from the Gospels, one for each week of our summer study, and asked different women in our congregation to speak. Some of the women who taught loved it and wanted to teach again sometime. Other women said thanks, but once was enough for them. Still, this allowed us to hear from more women, to glean from all the wisdom and experience stored up right there in our own congregation.

> Jesus's public ministry wasn't birthed on a grand stage.

I never started my own group of Inklings, but my dream to gather with women and magnify the name of Christ never went away either. My heart continued to beat with the desire to give women a voice and a chance to share their story. So I started to pray and ask God what it might look like to put Titus 2 into action. I dreamed of creating a space where women could connect with other women, and most importantly, connect with God. I dreamed of inviting women to stay connected in between those respites by staying in the Word.

The more I prayed, the more I kept thinking about the start of Jesus's ministry. As soon as He was baptized, the Spirit led Him to the wilderness, where He fasted for 40 days. The devil tempted Him, but Jesus rebutted every attempt by quoting Scripture. Soon thereafter, Jesus met some fishermen, and by the end of the day, He had asked Peter, Andrew, James, and John to follow Him.

> When He had finished speaking, He said to Simon, "Put out into deep water and let down your nets for a catch"...When they did this, they caught a great number of fish...Then they brought the boats to land, left everything, and followed Him (Luke 5:4-11).

Jesus's public ministry wasn't birthed on a grand stage. He was born in a stable. Then He spent 30 years in obscurity. After His baptism He spent more time in solitude, fasting and praying and overcoming temptation. His public ministry started by teaching those nearest Him, and then a few men started following Him.

As much as I wanted to bring women together, I had a string of doubts. What if they rejected me? What if I tried something and it was a total flop? The more I wrestled with this, the more I kept hearing these words from Scripture: "Put out into deep water" (Luke 5:4).

When Jesus asked the fishermen to put out into deep water, it didn't make sense because the fish swam in shallower water where it was warmer. The fishermen knew this. Trying to fish in deep water was illogical and futile. Besides, they'd been fishing for a while and had caught nothing. But they obeyed Jesus anyway and let down their nets in deeper water. The catch of fish was so huge they needed their partners in another boat to come help them out.

> It's there, in the stuff of everyday life, where we find the best reasons to laugh.

I never became a midwife, but I did come alongside women. Women who labor in a different way. Women who want to know God better through His Word. Women who want to share Him with other women. I invited my friends from Team 365 plus other women I knew to share their stories about faith and friendship, marriage and motherhood, on a website at www.deeperwaters.us. But I didn't want it to be just an online thing, because the image of that fallen ash tree stays with me. So I created a place—in real time and space—where we could gather. A women's retreat for anyone who thirsts to know Jesus more.

My heart's desire is to bring women together from all generations because I believe in the wisdom of Titus 2. At the first Deeper Waters Retreat, we had a few speakers, some with names you might recognize and some with names you wouldn't. I invited women from our local community to share their stories, women whose hearts shine for Jesus. I created a panel of women in local church leadership, too, and invited the attendees to submit questions. We had a panel discussion on everything from daily devotions to raising teenage sons.

> Invite women to gather. Not just to hear a speaker, but to hear each other.

My favorite part of the retreat was the laughter. Women say the funniest things. It's especially funny when you know it's not been scripted or rehearsed. We didn't have a professional comedian. We had real women with real stories, and it's there, in the stuff of everyday life, we find the best reasons to laugh.

I did something else too. I found some inexpensive lanterns for centerpieces. With a candle's flame inside each lantern, I wanted the tables to reflect the psalm that says, "Thy word is a lamp unto my feet, and a light unto my path."[2] The psalmist describes God's Word as a lamp, a guiding light. I wanted a "lamp" at the center of each round table to remind us that God's Word is the center of everything we do.

I share this because I'd love for women everywhere, if they're not already, to try something similar. To bring women together. Women from your own congregation. Form a panel of older women and invite the younger women in your church to submit questions. Form a panel of younger women and ask them what their needs are. Create a time when women of all ages in your church can share how they met Jesus. Invite women to gather. Not just to hear a speaker, but to hear each other.

I'm not suggesting we pass around a microphone at random. Prayerful discernment on the part of leadership is foundational. But I am suggesting we begin looking to the women around us, in our very own congregations, especially in age groups other than our own. Surely God has called more than one or two or three women to be voices of influence in our lives.

When Nehemiah inspects the reconstruction efforts around Jerusalem, he mentions the Nethinim people who made repairs in front of the Water Gate, which makes sense because that's where they worked.[3] The job

> We need more water bringers today.

of the Nethinim wasn't a glorious one. They were the equivalent of water boys at a football game.[4] Water boys are not the athletes on the field or the coaches commanding the game. They have a quiet but necessary job to do; they bring water to the football players. In a similar way, the Nethinim were the temple servants. They served the priests and Levites by bringing them water—because, you know, animal sacrifices could get kind of messy and bloody.

I daresay we need more water bringers today. We need more "water servants" in the body of Christ, those with a willing obedience to bring the water of the Word to the messy, bleeding hearts so in need of His life-changing truth.

> Ministry in deeper waters requires total trust and reliance on God.

That day I met Kay for lunch, I encouraged her to do two things: pray and start small. I encouraged her to find one young woman she could befriend—maybe someone she already had a relationship with. She could start there. She could begin investing in one woman. Also, a moms' group meets at our church. Maybe she could share her list of things that helped her as a mom with the moms who meet at church. Maybe she could volunteer to serve as a mentor mom.

That's how ministry begins. With one person. Then a few. Then a few more.

Ministry in deeper waters might not make sense at first. It might even seem foolish to the outside world. It will definitely require trust and total reliance on God.

I invite you to dive into deeper waters with me.

The Song We Sing

Sing praises to the LORD... Weeping may tarry for the night,
but joy comes with the morning.

PSALM 30:4-5 ESV

I tiptoe downstairs to steep a hot cup of morning tea before sitting down with my Bible. I'm reading through the Old Testament and I've reached the part in Lamentations where Jeremiah describes the Babylonian invasion. These are the first words I read:

> The Lord in his anger has cast a dark shadow over beautiful Jerusalem (Lamentations 2:1 NLT).

What a way to start the day. And it doesn't stop there. The scene that's described tears at the heart. It reads like something out of a tragic movie, but it's not a screenplay. This was real. They were real people. With names and friends and dreams. I turn the page and can hardly believe the following words.

> For many of us, the willows are all we know, and what we know oftentimes feels safer than what we don't know.

> Great is his faithfulness; his mercies begin afresh each morning (2:23 NLT).

The Lord's mercies are new every day. And yet, as often as I hear this verse quoted, I never hear anyone mention the devastation just a chapter before. How can the writer of Lamentations describe such horror and still look to the heavens and declare the Lord faithful and merciful?

Seventy years later, most Hebrews chose to stay in Babylon. I can understand why. Why return to Jerusalem to serve a God who didn't keep their ancestors safe? How could they trust God when He clearly allowed all manner of hatred and chaos to wreck their families' lives? Babylon wasn't great, but it's what they knew. One exile described their situation by penning these words:

> By the waters of Babylon, there we sat down and wept, when we remembered Zion.* On the willows there we hung up our lyres. For there our captors required of us songs, and our tormentors, mirth, saying, "Sing us one of the songs of Zion!" How shall we sing the Lord's song in a foreign land? (Psalm 137:1-4 ESV).

The Hebrews were known for their singing, and their captors taunted them with requests. But how could they sing after so much devastation and heartache? The psalmist in exile says they hung up their lyres on the willows. This was their way of saying they were done with singing and rejoicing, done with laughter and mirth. And they chose to stay by the willows.

> The first thing Ezra wants everyone to know—with the very first sentence he writes—is that God's Word can be trusted.

How many of us can relate? How many of us have hung up our lyres on our own willows? Hung up our dance shoes? Hung up our hopes? Hung up our dreams? For many of us, the willows are all we know, and what we know oftentimes feels safer than what we don't know. For me, it's not a question of

---

* Zion is another name for Jerusalem.

why so many exiles didn't return to Jerusalem, but why any returned at all. But Ezra explains why.

> In the first year of Cyrus king of Persia, the word of the LORD spoken through Jeremiah was fulfilled (Ezra 1:1).

The first thing Ezra wants everyone to know—with the very first sentence he writes—is that God's Word can be trusted. Remember Jeremiah's prophecy? "'I know the plans I have for you,' declares the LORD, 'plans to prosper you and not to harm you, plans to give you hope and a future'" (Jeremiah 29:11 NIV). Jeremiah said it. God did it. And Ezra reminds everyone of it.

Still, no matter how true this truth is, there are days when our lament lingers. When these moments come—and they surely do come—we're not left to thrash through the dark waves of suffering on our own. God has given us Himself. In His presence we find peace.

> When my lament is strong and my faith is weak, I reach for my Bible and pen to write the words of Scripture by hand.

So on those days when my lament is strong and my faith is weak, I reach for my Bible and pen to write the words of Scripture by hand. One verse, then another. Filling the pages until a chapter is finished. It's in these moments I must choose—whether I'm going to hold on to my lament and hang up my lyre on the willows or do the hard work of grieving and release my sorrow into the crimson hollow of my Savior's hands.

Every person's life is a song, and this song has a theme, whether we're a writer or a mechanic, a waiter or an accountant. The theme of a person's song is like a score of music that serves as a backdrop in a movie. It's there, almost imperceptible, but still present in every scene, lending itself to the whole of the story.

> Your statutes are the theme of my song during my earthly life (Psalm 119:54).

> Immersed in Scripture I write each word and meditate long— this is the theme of my song.

The theme of my song—the theme that pervades every scene of my life—is a deep love for God's Word. Where would I be without Him? Without His Word? I met the living God through the pages of His Word, and I want everyone to know the same saving grace, transforming power, and redeeming love.

> Go now, write it on a tablet for them, inscribe it on a scroll, that for the days to come it may be an everlasting witness (Isaiah 30:8 NIV).

A long time ago I adopted Isaiah 30:8 as my life verse—sort of like my own personal mission statement. For a life verse, this one may seem a bit peculiar. I doubt it makes the average top-ten list of favorite verses. When I read it for the first time, though, I immediately stopped reading. My intention of covering a few chapters during my quiet time suddenly took a different direction. I read the verse over and over again.

This has been the theme of my song for a very long time. For me, the scribbling and scribing never get old. I return often to the instructions Moses left for the kings that would one day preside over Israel:

> When [the king] is seated on his royal throne, he is to
> write a copy of this instruction for himself on a scroll in
> the presence of the Levitical priests. It is to remain with
> him, and he is to read from it all the days of his life (Deu-
> teronomy 17:18-19).

If copying Scripture by hand was good enough for the kings of
Israel, it's good enough for me. Immersed in Scripture I write each
word and meditate long. This is the theme of my song.

On his fifteenth birthday, Kendall walks up to me and gives me
a present. I'm confused. It's his birthday, not mine. Why give me a
gift? Kendall explains that our birthdays are exactly six months apart,
to the day. His birthday is my half-birthday. So he got me a gift with
his paper route money.

"Happy half-birthday, lil' sis!"

How many teenage boys spend their own money to buy their
little sister a present when it's his birthday? That's Kendall. Always
thinking of someone else. In thirty-five years since, hardly a half-
birthday has passed without one of us calling the other.

Kendall has continued to defy all odds. He lived when all the
doctors said he shouldn't be alive. He became the first person on
both sides of our family to earn a college degree. Then he went on
to earn three separate teaching credentials. Today he teaches high
school students with disabilities. He purchased some property and
had a brand new house built to accommodate his wheelchair. And
he refuses to let his limitations limit him.

He's been tandem skydiving and bungee jumping. Well, he
couldn't do the jumping part, but once they harnessed him in, they

pushed him over the edge. He loved it. Kendall also became a certi-fied scuba diver. (His legs proved problematic, though, because they kept floating to the surface. They needed to strap weights to his legs so he could stay underwater.) And you can't live in Northern California without tubing down the Sacramento River. Once he's on his tube, look out.

Kendall chooses life.

Of all the words Ezra recorded, these are my favorite:

> And now for a little space grace hath been shewed from the LORD our God, to leave us a remnant to escape...that our God may lighten our eyes, and give us a little reviving in our bondage (Ezra 9:8 KJV).

And now for a little space, for a brief moment, grace has been shown from the Lord our God.

While we wait with expectant hope for the future we have in Christ, for the new bodies we'll one day receive and the reunion with loved ones we'll one day share, God gives us a little space of grace, here and now. He blesses us with moments of respite. A chance to exhale. A reason to smile. The loss isn't erased. It's still there. But somehow, by God's grace, there are days when we're able to laugh at the hard anyway.

> While we wait with expectant hope...God gives us a little space of grace in the here and now.

After our daughter's fifth-grade colonial play, we drive to a frozen yogurt shop with another family whose daughter was also in the play. Our daughters are best friends. Her father is a police officer, but prior to that he spent 20 years in active military service. For a while there he was in Afghanistan and other places more than he was home, and sometimes he gets a faraway look in his eyes as though he's remembering another place, a place where war is everyday life. He's home now, but his fellow soldiers are still there, serving overseas. He knows firsthand there's a world far removed from this one here, where the biggest decision of the day is whether you should have gummy worms or cookie dough on your frozen yogurt.

My husband gets that faraway look too. It happens every December 8, when a radio disc jockey mentions the anniversary of John Lennon's death. On the day the world lost the Beatles icon, a ten-year-old boy in Oregon lost his dad. It's the kind of loss you never forget or get over, it's a loss that stays with you forever. But it feels extra cruel to have the radio remind you every year of the loss everyone else remembers, yet no one remembers your own.

That faraway look happens to me too. Sometimes when I least expect it. As I scoop broken bits of a Butterfinger onto my yogurt, I wonder how they're doing, the mummies from all those years ago. The burn victims whose space I once shared. Where are they now? Did they make it? Or did they make it to someplace far better? Then I wonder about those same halls now. Filled with new souls, and newly broken bodies. Not just there, but in hospitals everywhere. People are hurting right now, somewhere, while I munch on Butterfinger. It doesn't seem right. But it's a dissonance you learn to live with.

> That faraway look, that knowing of untold sorrow, it fades for the briefest moments, for a little space of grace.

Once the valley of the shadow of death has become your every-day norm, you learn to go through the motions, like brushing your teeth and tying your shoes. But the whole time it's as if a soundtrack is playing in the background you alone can hear; it's a melancholy refrain, a dissonant chord that refuses to resolve. After a while you get used to it. You learn to live in two worlds. The world where you still pump gas and pay the electric bill, and the world where you sit next to the dying and hold a straw while they drink from a tiny carton of milk. Then your son piles so many crumbs of Oreo cookies on top of his frozen yogurt you can't help but laugh at the sweetness that's as much in his heart as on his yogurt. And that faraway look, that knowing of untold sorrow, it fades for the briefest moment, for a little space of grace.

Starting Today

Read it. Write it. Pray it.

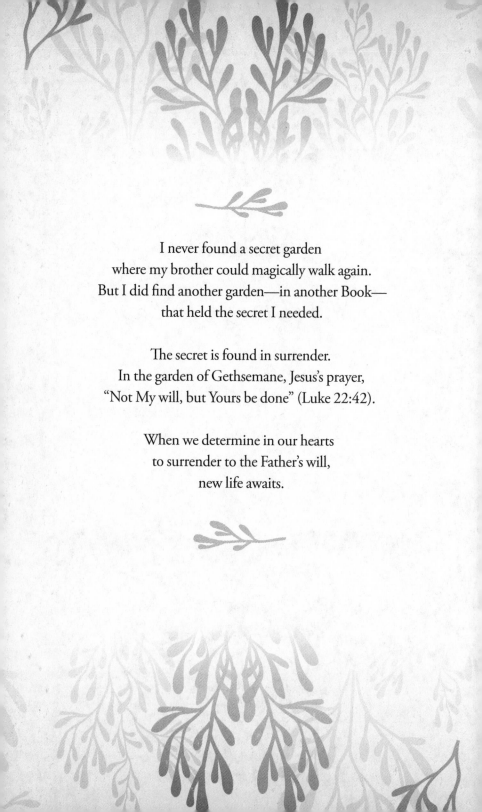

I never found a secret garden
where my brother could magically walk again.
But I did find another garden—in another Book—
that held the secret I needed.

The secret is found in surrender.
In the garden of Gethsemane, Jesus's prayer,
"Not My will, but Yours be done" (Luke 22:42).

When we determine in our hearts
to surrender to the Father's will,
new life awaits.

Read It

When I'm involved in a Bible study at church, I get into a groove. I buy the workbook and join a group. Being with other women who are doing the same study creates accountability. We make a commitment to show up each week with our homework finished. It works for me.

When the study session ends, I'll do okay for a while, reading a few psalms here and few parables there. But after a while my fervor wanes. Without a plan, my daily quiet time turns into a weekly quiet time. Or worse.

To remedy this, I bought a Bible with 365 readings, where each day included a little bit of Old Testament, a little bit of New Testament, and a few Psalms and Proverbs sprinkled in for good measure—like salt and pepper on your meat and potatoes. It was a nice idea, but it didn't work, at least not for me. The text didn't flow because the stories were chopped in strange places. I'd start to get into a passage, then the plan redirected my reading elsewhere. I found the experience frustrating and quit. Then I felt guilty for quitting.

I don't think I'm alone either. Most people experience ups and downs in their quiet times. I've noticed, however, that my dry seasons all had one thing in common: I lacked a reading plan.

For me, the antidote for a lapse in daily Bible study is to have a reading plan. That way I'm not coming to the Bible each day wondering what I should read. I'm not flipping and skipping until I find something that strikes my fancy. Nor am I opening up to a random page and starting wherever. Just imagine trying to read Shakespeare that way! As an English teacher, I would never tell my students to open up a Shakespearean play in the middle, read a few lines, and call it good for the day. They'd never learn how the scenes work together for the overall plot. Having a plan remedies this typical plight-of-the-random-quiet-time.

The most promising way to stay in God's Word daily is to move through the books of the Bible, not hopscotching our way through, landing on some parts and skipping others. Below you'll find a reading plan that takes you through the Bible, from Genesis through Revelation, by reading three or four chapters a day for one year.

With this plan you can read the book of Judges in seven days because Judges has 21 chapters, and that's three chapters a day. But maybe you want to spend more time in Judges. That's great too. Or perhaps you want to focus on reading through the New Testament. This plan leads you through the New Testament in 90 days. That's just three months! Maybe you want to take things slower and finish the reading plan in two years, or three. Find the pace that works for you and commit to it.

In chapter 7, we talked about the time we spend in God's Word. Here you'll find a quick synopsis of those key points:

1. Prayerfully select a book of the Bible to study. (The Gospel of John is always a great place to begin!) If your Bible has an introduction to the book, read it first.

2. Before reading, pray this simple prayer from Psalm 119:18: "Open my eyes that I may see wonderful things in your law" (NIV).

3. Read the book straight through, from start to finish. Depending on its length and the pace you choose, this may be possible in one sitting, or it may take a few days. Ask God to reveal Himself to you as you read His Word. Underline any passages that stand out to you. Write any questions you have in the margins.

4. Once you finish, go back to the first chapter. Read just the first chapter, or maybe just a larger passage within the first chapter. Look for verses that do the following:

   - Declare a truth.

   - Give a command.

   - Post a warning.

   - Present a promise.

   - Share a prayer.

   - Offer an example.

5. Look up any cross references your Bible gives. Try reading the same passage in another version too.

6. Once you finish a passage or a chapter, select a verse or two and write them in a journal or notebook. Talk to God about the passage you've read. Ask Him how He wants you to respond to it.

7. Finish your time in the Word the same way you began— with prayer.

Move through each passage or chapter in this way.

365-Day Bible Reading Plan

Day		Book of the Old Testament
16 Days of Genesis		
1	1	Genesis 1-3
2	2	Genesis 4-6
3	3	Genesis 7-9
4	4	Genesis 10-12
5	5	Genesis 13-15
6	6	Genesis 16-18
7	7	Genesis 19-21
8	8	Genesis 22-25
9	9	Genesis 26-28
10	10	Genesis 29-31
11	11	Genesis 32-34
12	12	Genesis 35-37
13	13	Genesis 38-40
14	14	Genesis 41-43
15	15	Genesis 44-47
16	16	Genesis 48-50
12 Days of Exodus		
17	1	Exodus 1-3
18	2	Exodus 4-7
19	3	Exodus 8-10
20	4	Exodus 11-14

Day		Book of the Old Testament
21	5	Exodus 15-17
22	6	Exodus 18-21
23	7	Exodus 22-24
24	8	Exodus 25-28
25	9	Exodus 29-31
26	10	Exodus 32-34
27	11	Exodus 35-37
28	12	Exodus 38-40
9 Days of Leviticus		
29	1	Leviticus 1-3
30	2	Leviticus 4-6
31	3	Leviticus 7-9
32	4	Leviticus 10-12
33	5	Leviticus 13-15
34	6	Leviticus 16-18
35	7	Leviticus 19-21
36	8	Leviticus 22-24
37	9	Leviticus 25-27
12 Days of Numbers		
38	1	Numbers 1-3
39	2	Numbers 4-6
40	3	Numbers 7-9

Day		Book of the Old Testament	Day		Book of the Old Testament
41	4	Numbers 10-12	64	4	Joshua 11-13
42	5	Numbers 13-15	65	5	Joshua 14-17
43	6	Numbers 16-18	66	6	Joshua 18-21
44	7	Numbers 19-21	67	7	Joshua 22-24
45	8	Numbers 22-24	*7 Days of Judges*		
46	9	Numbers 25-27	68	1	Judges 1-3
47	10	Numbers 28-30	69	2	Judges 4-6
48	11	Numbers 31-33	70	3	Judges 7-9
49	12	Numbers 34-36	71	4	Judges 10-12
11 Days of Deuteronomy			72	5	Judges 13-15
50	1	Deuteronomy 1-3	73	6	Judges 16-18
51	2	Deuteronomy 4-6	74	7	Judges 19-21
52	3	Deuteronomy 7-9	*1 Day of Ruth*		
53	4	Deuteronomy 10-12	75	1	Ruth 1-4
54	5	Deuteronomy 13-16	*9 Days of 1 Samuel*		
55	6	Deuteronomy 17-19	76	1	1 Samuel 1-3
56	7	Deuteronomy 20-22	77	2	1 Samuel 4-7
57	8	Deuteronomy 23-25	78	3	1 Samuel 8-11
58	9	Deuteronomy 26-28	79	4	1 Samuel 12-14
59	10	Deuteronomy 29-31	80	5	1 Samuel 15-17
60	11	Deuteronomy 32-34	81	6	1 Samuel 18-20
7 Days of Joshua			82	7	1 Samuel 21-24
61	1	Joshua 1-4	83	8	1 Samuel 25-27
62	2	Joshua 5-7	84	9	1 Samuel 28-31
63	3	Joshua 8-10	*7 Days of 2 Samuel*		

Day		Book of the Old Testament	Day		Book of the Old Testament
85	1	2 Samuel 1-3	108	3	1 Chronicles 9-11
86	2	2 Samuel 4-6	109	4	1 Chronicles 12-14
87	3	2 Samuel 7-10	110	5	1 Chronicles 15-17
88	4	2 Samuel 11-13	111	6	1 Chronicles 18-20
89	5	2 Samuel 14-16	112	7	1 Chronicles 21-23
90	6	2 Samuel 17-20	113	8	1 Chronicles 24-26
91	7	2 Samuel 21-24	114	9	1 Chronicles 27-29
7 Days of 1 Kings			*10 Days of 2 Chronicles*		
92	1	1 Kings 1-3	115	1	2 Chronicles 1-3
93	2	1 Kings 4-6	116	2	2 Chronicles 4-6
94	3	1 Kings 7-9	117	3	2 Chronicles 7-10
95	4	1 Kings 10-12	118	4	2 Chronicles 11-13
96	5	1 Kings 13-15	119	5	2 Chronicles 14-17
97	6	1 Kings 16-19	120	6	2 Chronicles 18-21
98	7	1 Kings 20-22	121	7	2 Chronicles 22-25
7 Days of 2 Kings			122	8	2 Chronicles 26-29
99	1	2 Kings 1-3	123	9	2 Chronicles 30-33
100	2	2 Kings 4-6	124	10	2 Chronicles 34-36
101	3	2 Kings 7-9	*3 Days of Ezra*		
102	4	2 Kings 10-13	125	1	Ezra 1-3
103	5	2 Kings 14-17	126	2	Ezra 4-6
104	6	2 Kings 18-21	127	3	Ezra 7-10
105	7	2 Kings 22-25	*4 Days of Nehemiah*		
9 Days of 1 Chronicles			128	1	Nehemiah 1-3
106	1	1 Chronicles 1-4	129	2	Nehemiah 4-7
107	2	1 Chronicles 5-8	130	3	Nehemiah 8-10

Day		Book of the Old Testament	Day		Book of the Old Testament
131	4	Nehemiah 11-13	154	8	Psalms 31-34
	3 Days of Esther		155	9	Psalms 35-37
132	1	Esther 1-3	156	10	Psalms 38-41
133	2	Esther 4-7	157	11	Psalms 42-45
134	3	Esther 8-10	158	12	Psalms 46-49
	12 Days of Job		159	13	Psalms 50-53
135	1	Job 1-3	160	14	Psalms 54-57
136	2	Job 4-7	161	15	Psalms 58-61
137	3	Job 8-10	162	16	Psalms 62-65
138	4	Job 11-14	163	17	Psalms 66-69
139	5	Job 15-18	164	18	Psalms 70-73
140	6	Job 19-21	165	19	Psalms 74-77
141	7	Job 22-25	166	20	Psalms 78-80
142	8	Job 26-29	167	21	Psalms 81-84
143	9	Job 30-32	168	22	Psalms 85-88
144	10	Job 33-35	169	23	Psalms 89-91
145	11	Job 36-38	170	24	Psalms 92-95
146	12	Job 39-42	171	25	Psalms 96-99
	38 Days of Psalms		172	26	Psalms 100-103
147	1	Psalms 1-5	173	27	Psalms 104-106
148	2	Psalms 6-9	174	28	Psalms 107-109
149	3	Psalms 10-14	175	29	Psalms 110-114
150	4	Psalms 15-18	176	30	Psalms 115-118
151	5	Psalms 19-22	177	31	Psalm 119
152	6	Psalms 23-26	178	32	Psalms 120-125
153	7	Psalms 27-30	179	33	Psalms 126-130

Day		Book of the Old Testament	Day		Book of the Old Testament
180	34	Psalms 131-135	202	3	Isaiah 7-9
181	35	Psalms 136-139	203	4	Isaiah 10-12
182	36	Psalms 140-143	204	5	Isaiah 13-15
183	37	Psalms 144-146	205	6	Isaiah 16-18
184	38	Psalms 147-150	206	7	Isaiah 19-21
		9 Days of Proverbs	207	8	Isaiah 22-24
185	1	Proverbs 1-3	208	9	Isaiah 25-27
186	2	Proverbs 4-7	209	10	Isaiah 28-30
187	3	Proverbs 8-10	210	11	Isaiah 31-33
188	4	Proverbs 11-13	211	12	Isaiah 34-36
189	5	Proverbs 14-16	212	13	Isaiah 37-39
190	6	Proverbs 17-19	213	14	Isaiah 40-42
191	7	Proverbs 20-23	214	15	Isaiah 43-45
192	8	Proverbs 24-27	215	16	Isaiah 46-48
193	9	Proverbs 28-31	216	17	Isaiah 49-51
		4 Days of Ecclesiastes	217	18	Isaiah 52-54
194	1	Ecclesiastes 1-3	218	19	Isaiah 55-57
195	2	Ecclesiastes 4-6	219	20	Isaiah 58-60
196	3	Ecclesiastes 7-9	220	21	Isaiah 61-63
197	4	Ecclesiastes 10-12	221	22	Isaiah 64-66
		2 Days of Song of Songs			*17 Days of Jeremiah*
198	1	Song of Songs 1-4	222	1	Jeremiah 1-3
199	2	Song of Songs 5-8	223	2	Jeremiah 4-6
		22 Days of Isaiah	224	3	Jeremiah 7-9
200	1	Isaiah 1-3	225	4	Jeremiah 10-12
201	2	Isaiah 4-6	226	5	Jeremiah 13-15

Day		Book of the Old Testament	Day		Book of the Old Testament
227	6	Jeremiah 16-18	250	10	Ezekiel 37-40
228	7	Jeremiah 19-21	251	11	Ezekiel 41-44
229	8	Jeremiah 22-24	252	12	Ezekiel 45-48
230	9	Jeremiah 25-27	*4 Days of Daniel*		
231	10	Jeremiah 28-31	253	1	Daniel 1-3
232	11	Jeremiah 32-34	254	2	Daniel 4-6
233	12	Jeremiah 35-37	255	3	Daniel 7-9
234	13	Jeremiah 38-40	256	4	Daniel 10-12
235	14	Jeremiah 41-44	*4 Days of Hosea*		
236	15	Jeremiah 45-48	257	1	Hosea 1-3
237	16	Jeremiah 49-50	258	2	Hosea 4-6
238	17	Jeremiah 51-52	259	3	Hosea 7-10
2 Days of Lamentations			260	4	Hosea 11-14
239	1	Lamentations 1-2	*1 Day of Joel*		
240	2	Lamentations 3-5	261	1	Joel 1-3
12 Days of Ezekiel			*2 Days of Amos*		
241	1	Ezekiel 1-4	262	1	Amos 1-4
242	2	Ezekiel 5-8	263	2	Amos 5-9
243	3	Ezekiel 9-12	*1 Day of Obadiah*		
244	4	Ezekiel 13-16	264	1	Obadiah 1
245	5	Ezekiel 17-20	*1 Day of Jonah*		
246	6	Ezekiel 21-24	265	1	Jonah 1-4
247	7	Ezekiel 25-28	*2 Days of Micah*		
248	8	Ezekiel 29-32	266	1	Micah 1-4
249	9	Ezekiel 33-36	267	2	Micah 5-7

Day		Book of the Old Testament	Day		Book of the New Testament
	1 Day of Nahum		285	10	Matthew 25-26
268	1	Nahum 1-3	286	11	Matthew 27-28
	1 Day of Habakkuk			*7 Days of Mark*	
269	1	Habakkuk 1-3	287	1	Mark 1-3
	1 Day of Zephaniah		288	2	Mark 4-5
270	1	Zephaniah 1-3	289	3	Mark 6-7
	1 Day of Haggai		290	4	Mark 8-9
271	1	Haggai 1-2	291	5	Mark 10-11
	3 Days of Zechariah		292	6	Mark 12-13
272	1	Zechariah 1-5	293	7	Mark 14-16
273	2	Zechariah 6-10		*11 Days of Luke*	
274	3	Zechariah 11-14	294	1	Luke 1-2
	1 Days of Malachi		295	2	Luke 3-4
275	1	Malachi 1-4	296	3	Luke 5-6
Day		Book of the New Testament	297	4	Luke 7-8
			298	5	Luke 9-10
	11 Days of Matthew		299	6	Luke 11-12
276	1	Matthew 1-3	300	7	Luke 13-15
277	2	Matthew 4-6	301	8	Luke 16-18
278	3	Matthew 7-9	302	9	Luke 19-20
279	4	Matthew 10-12	303	10	Luke 21-22
280	5	Matthew 13-15	304	11	Luke 23-24
281	6	Matthew 16-18		*7 Days of John*	
282	7	Matthew 19-20	305	1	John 1-3
283	8	Matthew 21-22	306	2	John 4-6
284	9	Matthew 23-24	307	3	John 7-9

Day		Book of the New Testament
308	4	John 10-12
309	5	John 13-15
310	6	John 16-18
311	7	John 19-21
10 Days of Acts		
312	1	Acts 1-3
313	2	Acts 4-6
314	3	Acts 7-9
315	4	Acts 10-12
316	5	Acts 13-15
317	6	Acts 16-18
318	7	Acts 19-21
319	8	Acts 22-24
320	9	Acts 25-26
321	10	Acts 27-28
4 Days of Romans		
322	1	Romans 1-4
323	2	Romans 5-8
324	3	Romans 9-12
325	4	Romans 13-16
4 Days of 1 Corinthians		
326	1	1 Corinthians 1-4
327	2	1 Corinthians 5-8
328	3	1 Corinthians 9-12
329	4	1 Corinthians 13-16
3 Days of 2 Corinthians		

Day		Book of the New Testament
330	1	2 Corinthians 1-4
331	2	2 Corinthians 5-9
332	3	2 Corinthians 10-13
2 Days of Galatians		
333	1	Galatians 1-3
334	2	Galatians 4-6
2 Days of Ephesians		
335	1	Ephesians 1-3
336	2	Ephesians 4-6
1 Day of Philippians		
337	1	Philippians 1-4
1 Day of Colossians		
338	1	Colossians 1-4
2 Days of 1 Thessalonians		
339	1	1 Thessalonians 1-3
340	2	1 Thessalonians 4-5
1 Day of 2 Thessalonians		
341	1	2 Thessalonians 1-3
2 Days of 1 Timothy		
342	1	1 Timothy 1-3
343	2	1 Timothy 4-5
1 Day of 2 Timothy		
344	1	2 Timothy 1-4
1 Day of Titus & Philemon		
345	1	Titus 1-3 & Philemon 1

Day		Book of the New Testament	Day		Book of the New Testament
5 Days of Hebrews			**2 Days of 1 John**		
346	1	Hebrews 1-3	356	1	1 John 1-3
347	2	Hebrews 4-6	357	2	1 John 4-5
348	3	Hebrews 7-9	**1 Day of 2, 3 John & Jude**		
349	4	Hebrews 10-11	358	1	2, 3 John & Jude
350	5	Hebrews 12-13	**7 Days of Revelation**		
2 Days of James			359	1	Revelation 1-3
351	1	James 1-2	360	2	Revelation 4-7
352	2	James 3-5	361	3	Revelation 8-10
2 Days of 1 Peter			362	4	Revelation 11-13
353	1	1 Peter 1-2	363	5	Revelation 14-16
354	2	1 Peter 3-5	364	6	Revelation 17-19
1 Day of 2 Peter			365	7	Revelation 20-22
355	1	2 Peter 1-3			

Write It

Ezra is one of my favorite people in Scripture. He determined in his heart to study God's Word, to obey God's voice, and to teach God's precepts. I want to do the same, because genuine transformation only happens when we're immersed in the grace and truth of God's Word. On the lined pages that follow, you're invited to join the rich heritage of Ezra and the scribes and become a Word Writer yourself. A beautiful space has been created for you to write out Psalm 119 from your favorite Bible translation.

Psalm 119 is a work solely about the Word of God. Some scholars speculate that David may have authored this psalm; more recent scholarship, however, makes an equally strong case for an author from the post-exilic period—with the most likely candidate being Ezra. He devoted his life to studying, obeying, teaching, and preserving God's Word. But nobody really knows who authored this psalm. What's more important is the psalm's content. It's all about the Word.

As you write each verse from this psalm, ask God to birth in you a deeper passion for His Word. Ask God to reveal Himself to you through the truth and beauty of Scripture. Ask Him to speak to you through His Word. The fruit of studying and obeying God's Word is that we become more like Christ. When we immerse ourselves in Scripture and follow its precepts, we reflect God's heart in our interactions with others as we traverse this earth toward our true home in God's presence.

Psalm 119

verses 1-8

Psalm 119:9-16

Psalm 119:17-24

Psalm 119:25-32

Psalm 119:33-40

Psalm 119:41-48

Psalm 119:49-56

Psalm 119:57-64

Psalm 119:65-72

Psalm 119:73-80

Psalm 119:81-88

Psalm 119:89-96

Psalm 119:97-104

Psalm 119:105-112

Psalm 119:113-120

Psalm 119:121-128

Psalm 119:129-136

Psalm 119:137-144

Psalm 119:145-152

Psalm 119:153-160

Psalm 119:161-168

Psalm 119:169-176

Pray It

When we pray the words of Scripture, we can trust we're praying according to God's will. Here are just a few of my favorite prayers from Scripture I pray often. As you're reading God's Word, make note of the prayers you come across and make them your own.

Prayers of Jesus

Our Father in heaven, Your name be honored as holy. Your kingdom come. Your will be done on earth as it is in heaven. Give us today our daily bread. And forgive us our debts, as we also have forgiven our debtors. And do not bring us into temptation, but deliver us from the evil one. [For Yours is the kingdom and the power and the glory forever. Amen] (Matthew 9:8-13).

Father, I thank You that You heard Me. I know that You always hear Me (John 11:41-42).

Father, if You are willing, take this cup away from Me—nevertheless not My will, but Yours, be done (Luke 22:42).

A Prayer of Hannah

My heart rejoices in the LORD! The LORD has made me strong. Now I have an answer for my enemies; I rejoice because you rescued me. No one is holy like the LORD! There is no one besides you; there is no Rock like our God (1 Samuel 2:1-2 NLT).

A Prayer of Nehemiah

Praise Your glorious name, and may it be exalted above all blessing and praise. You alone are Yahweh. You created the heavens, the highest heavens with all their host, the earth and all that is on it, the seas and all that is in them. You give life to all of them, and the heavenly host worships You (Nehemiah 9:5-6).

A Prayer of Daniel

Listen, my God, and hear. Open Your eyes and see our desolations and the city called by Your name. For we are not presenting our petitions before You based on our righteous acts, but based on Your abundant compassion. Lord, hear! Lord, forgive! Lord, listen and act! My God, for Your own sake, do not delay, because Your city and Your people are called by Your name (Daniel 9:18-19).

A Prayer of Habakkuk

LORD, I have heard the report about You; LORD, I stand in awe of Your deeds. Revive Your work in these years; make it known in these years. In Your wrath remember mercy! (Habakkuk 3:2).

A Prayer of Samuel

Speak, for Your servant is listening (1 Samuel 3:10).

Prayers from the Psalms

You, LORD, are a shield around me, my glory, and the One who lifts up my head. I cry aloud to the LORD, and He answers me from His holy mountain. I lie down and sleep; I wake again because the LORD sustains me (Psalm 3:3-5).

May the words of my mouth and the meditation of my heart be acceptable to You, Lord, my rock and my Redeemer (Psalm 19:14).

Make Your ways known to me, Lord; teach me Your paths. Guide me in Your truth and teach me, for You are the God of my salvation (Psalm 25:4-5).

God, create a clean heart for me and renew a steadfast spirit within me. Do not banish me from Your presence or take Your Holy Spirit from me. Restore the joy of Your salvation to me, and give me a willing spirit (Psalm 51:10-12).

Search me, God, and know my heart; test me and know my anxious thoughts. See if there is any offensive way in me, and lead me in the way everlasting (Psalm 139:23-24 NIV).

I will exalt you, my God the King; I will praise your name for ever and ever. Every day I will praise you and extol your name for ever and ever. Great is the Lord and most worthy of praise; his greatness no one can fathom. One generation commends your works to another; they tell of your mighty acts. They speak of the glorious splendor of your majesty—and I will meditate on your wonderful works. They tell of the power of your awesome works—and I will proclaim your great deeds (Psalm 145:1-6 NIV).

Prayers of Paul

Praise the God and Father of our Lord Jesus Christ, the Father of mercies and the God of all comfort. He comforts us in all our affliction, so that we may be able to comfort those who are in any kind of affliction, through the comfort we ourselves receive from God (2 Corinthians 1:3-4).

Praise the God and Father of our Lord Jesus Christ, who has blessed us in Christ with every spiritual blessing in the heavens. For

He chose us in Him, before the foundation of the world, to be holy and blameless in His sight. In love He predestined us to be adopted through Jesus Christ for Himself, according to His favor and will, to the praise of His glorious grace that He favored us with in the Beloved (Ephesians 1:3-6).

A Prayer of Hezekiah

LORD God of Israel who is enthroned above the cherubim, You are God—You alone—of all the kingdoms of the earth. You made the heavens and the earth. Listen closely, LORD, and hear; open Your eyes, LORD, and see (2 Kings 19:15-16).

A Prayer of Jeremiah

Heal me, LORD, and I will be healed; save me, and I will be saved, for You are my praise (Jeremiah 17:14).

Prayers of Isaiah

Yahweh, You are my God; I will exalt You. I will praise Your name, for You have accomplished wonders, plans formed long ago, with perfect faithfulness (Isaiah 25:1).

You will keep the mind that is dependent on You in perfect peace, for it is trusting in You (Isaiah 26:3).

A Prayer of Ezra

And now for a little space grace hath been shewed from the LORD our God, to leave us a remnant to escape...that our God may lighten our eyes, and give us a little reviving in our bondage (Ezra 9:8 KJV).

Notes

Part One—The Voice We Hear

1. When I refer to my "Activation Day"—the first time I distinctly heard my Father speak to me through the pages of His Word—I use that term because that's what my friends called the day they turned on their son's "new ears" after he received cochlear implants. In a similar way, many believers can pinpoint exactly where they were and what they were doing the first time they heard God speak to them through Scripture. Like Saul on the road to Damascus, a specific day and time changed the trajectory of their entire lives. But some believers may not be able to pinpoint an exact day and time, and that's okay too. This is especially true if someone grew up in the church.

2. McGee, J. Vernon, *Ezra, Nehemiah, Esther: History of Israel* (Nashville, TN: Thomas Nelson, 1997), vii.

3. Jeremiah 4:1-8.

4. Whitney, Donald S., *Spiritual Disciplines for the Christian Life*, Revised, Updated Edition (Carol Stream, IL: NavPress, 2014), 31.

Chapter 1—Exile We Know

1. Billy Graham Crusades were not billed as "healing crusades."

2. Wiersbe, Warren W., *Be Heroic*, Second Edition (Colorado Springs, CO: David C Cook, 2011), 52.

3. See Ezra 7:6.

Chapter 2—The Lament We Feel

1. Matthew 27:46.

Chapter 3—The Decision We Make

1. James 2:19.

2. Nehemiah 8:1-3.

3. Peterson, Eugene H., *Eat This Book* (Grand Rapids, MI: Eerdmans, 2009), 125.

Chapter 4—The Challenges We Face

1. 1 Samuel 3:10.

Part Two—To Study God's Word

Chapter 5— The Water We Need

1. Wiersbe, Warren W., *Be Determined* (Colorado Springs, CO: David C Cook, 2009), 53.

2. Exodus 20:3.

3. John 8:32.

Chapter 6—The Way We Wait

1. Piper, John, *A Peculiar Glory: How the Christian Scriptures Reveal Their Complete Truthfulness* (Wheaton, IL: Crossway, 2016), 213.

2. Genesis 2:8-9,16-17.

3. Genesis 4:3-5.

Chapter 7—The Time We Spend

1. Arthur, Kay, David Arthur, Pete DeLacy. *How to Study Your Bible: Discover the Life-Changing Approach to God's Word.* (Eugene, OR: Harvest House Publishers, 2010), ch. 6.

2. Isaiah 55:11 NKJV.

3. James 1:23-25.

Chapter 8—The Words We Write

1. Plato, *Phaedrus.*

2. http://www.nytimes.com/2014/06/03/science/whats-lost-as-handwriting-fades.html

3. https://www.washingtonpost.com/local/education/cursive-handwriting-disappearing-from-public-schools/2013/04/04/215862e0-7d23-11e2-a044-676856536b40_story.html?utm_term=.cccfe849d840

4. https://www.scientificamerican.com/article/a-learning-secret-don-t-take-notes-with-a-laptop/

5. 1 Samuel 16:23.

Chapter 9—The Prayers We Keep

1. 1 Samuel 3:9.

2. Romans 3:23.

3. Hebrews 4:16.

4. James 4:8.

5. Ezekiel 36:26.

6. Psalm 37:4.

7. Philippians 4:7.

Part Three—To Obey God's Voice

Chapter 10—The Truth We Live

1. Mark 12:30-31.

2. Haggai 1:4 NLT.

3. Murray, Andrew, *A Life of Obedience: Learning to Trust His Time, His Place, His Will* (Minneapolis, MN: Bethany House Publishers, 2004), 1.

4. Hebrews 12:2 ESV.

5. Galatians 1:6-9 ESV.

Chapter 11—The Compass We Follow

1. John 8:1-11 NLT.

2. Alcorn, Randy, *The Grace and Truth Paradox: Responding with Christlike Balance* (Sisters, OR: Multnomah, 2003), 87.

3. Matthew 5:21-22.

4. Alcorn, *The Grace and Truth Paradox*, 16.

5. Alcorn, *The Grace and Truth Paradox*, 13.

6. McGee, J. Vernon, *Thru the Bible Commentary Series: Psalms Chapters 90–150* (Nashville, TN: Thomas Nelson, 1997), 146.

7. Alcorn, *The Grace and Truth Paradox*, 88.

Chapter 12—The Failure We Grieve

1. Psalm 84:10 NIV.

2. James 2:10.

3. On April 10, 1912, the *Titanic* departed from England and embarked on its first and only voyage. Four days later the *Titanic* received seven separate warnings from other eastbound ships in the area. Their messages included the longitude and latitude of icebergs they'd seen in the sea lanes, but the *Titanic* refused to slow down. At the same time, the temperature of the water dropped from 43 to 31 degrees—a sure sign that ice was in the water. Thirty-seven seconds before impact, the lookout aboard the *Titanic* saw the foreboding iceberg and tried to turn the ship, but it was too late. His ill-fated decision resulted in the iceberg puncturing the entire length of the ship's side. If the ship had hit the iceberg head-on, they would have needed another ship to come and take the passengers, but the *Titanic* would not have sunk. http://www.titanicfacts.net/titanic-timeline.html

Chapter 13—The Purpose We Reclaim

1. John 21:1-9.

2. Genesis 37-50.

3. Ezra 7:1.

4. 2 Chronicles 34:14.

5. Joel 2:25 NIV.

6. Isaiah 55:9.

Chapter 14—The Grace We Give

1. Luke 12:48.

2. Peterson, Eugene H., *Answering God: The Psalms as Tools for Prayer* (San Francisco, CA: Harper-One, 1991), 98.

3. Psalm 103:12.

4. Genesis 9:1.

Part Four—To Teach God's Precepts

Chapter 15—The Women We Welcome

1. Hebrews 10:25.

2. 1 Thessalonians 5:11.

3. John 4:1-42.

Chapter 16—The Roots We Plant

1. 2 Corinthians 5:17-20.

Chapter 17—The Story We Share

1. Matthew 18:20.

2. Psalm 119:105 KJV.

3. Nehemiah 3:26.

4. McGee, J. Vernon, *Ezra, Nehemiah, Esther: History of Israel* (Nashville, TN: Thomas Nelson, 1997), 99.

Acknowledgments

I used to think books were made with words. But now I know books are made with people. And these are the people who have been a very special part of the story on these pages.

Team 365, you are the beautiful souls who braved to read the entire chronological Bible with me and other women around the country. Whenever I think of the many gifts the online world has brought me, you are at the top of my list.

My sisters at Deeper Waters, you have been with me from the beginning—sharing in this crazy dream to create a place, both online and in real space and time, for women to gather.

The team at (in)courage and DaySpring, you have welcomed me and embraced me and allowed me to share in the giving of words and encouragement with you. The ability to do what we do is a gift I treasure.

Terry Glaspey, I'm so grateful our paths crossed "by chance" on a rainy March morning in Oregon. Without your vision the words on these pages might never have made their way beyond my little desk in the corner of a crowded room. The two words *thank you* don't seem sufficient, but for now I pray they will do. Thank you.

LaRae Weikert, thank you for reaching out to me. Without your resolve this journey would not have come to fruition as it has, and I am most grateful.

Betty Fletcher, working with you has been a delight beyond words. I tell everyone I know I consider my editor a dear friend for life. I sure hope I get to hug you in person someday.

Bob Hawkins Jr., Kathleen Kerr, and the whole team at Harvest House—my sincerest thanks to all who work so tirelessly behind the scenes, making books and dreams.

Cheri Gregory, sometimes it's one conversation that turns the tide of a person's life. You will always be one of those tide-turning friends to me.

Steve Laube, I am forever grateful for your wisdom, your insight, and your many anecdotes for life and writing. So grateful indeed.

And to every Word Writer near and far, your emails, texts, voxes, and direct messages are like a beautiful quilt, warming me through with a kindness I can never forget.

Kendall, thank you for reading an early manuscript and sharing your thoughts and memories to make the words on these pages accurate. Your zest for life is unmatchable. You insist on seeing the glass half full. You are the most contagiously optimistic person I know. And I'm so blessed to call you brother and friend.

Simone, Brynn, and Parker—you three are my best three reasons for writing. When I think of all the things I'm passing on to you—like tea and Devonshire cream in Pasadena, red velvet cake on Christmas Day, and loud football games on Sunday afternoons—I pray the one thing I pass on best is a deep, abiding love for God's Word. May His voice guide you always.

Jeffrey, the best gift you've given me is the ability to laugh, and on the best days to laugh at myself. I love that I get to laugh through the days with you.

Jesus, where would I be without You? Without the Word made flesh? I shudder at the thought. Anything good—whether in me or from me or around me—is all because of You.

About the Author

Denise loves the world of words, where life and literature connect, but she's most passionate about the Book with living words—the Word of God. She's the author of Word Writers, a Bible study series that guides readers through individual books of the Bible, verse by verse, and then invites them to write out Scripture. She's also the Editorial Coordinator for (in)courage and the host of the Deeper Waters Retreat, where women can gather and grow deeper in God's Word. Denise lives with her husband and three kids in Southern California, where she reads three things every day—the Bible, nfl.com, and packers.com—sometimes in that order.

You can find Denise at:
www.DeniseJHughes.com
INSTAGRAM: @DeniseJHughes
TWITTER: @DeniseJHughes
FACEBOOK: /DeniseJHughes

You can find a community of
Truth Readers and Word Writers at:
www.DeeperWaters.us

Word Writers

EXPERIENCE THE BIBLE...WRITING WORD BY WORD

Word Writers
Philippians
Denise J. Hughes

Word Writers
Ephesians
Denise J. Hughes

Word Writers
James
Denise J. Hughes

Learn more at:
www.WordWriters.us

To learn more about Harvest House books and
to read sample chapters, visit our website:

www.harvesthousepublishers.com

HARVEST HOUSE PUBLISHERS
EUGENE, OREGON